AF442233

DARK PSYCHOLOGY SECRETS

23 powerful Techniques For Persuading and Influencing People with Mental Manipulation and NLP. Increase Your Conversation Capacity and Learn How to Deep Control People Mind.

By

Leonard Mind

To G.G.

TABLE OF CONTENTS

- o Technique 9: Playing with Emotions
- o Technique 10: How to Magnify the Problems in the right way
- o Technique 11: Illusion of choice
- o Technique 12: The simplicity is the key
- o Technique 13: The power of Touch
- o Technique 14: How to be Silent sometimes
- o Technique 15: Do it gradually
- o Technique 16: Repeat some words
- o Technique 17: Using empath skills
- o Technique 18: How to use Deception
- o Technique 19: Use the right Gestures
- o Technique 20: How to use Charism
- o Technique 21: How to use Leadership
- o Technique 22: Fake it until you make it
- o Technique 23: Never stop train yourself

5. The basics of Deception

6. BONUS: Tips from the author's experience

Conclusion

INTRODUCTION

Dark psychology: it isn't something that just appeared recently. Since it has a long history, what differentiates the present dark psychology to the past dark psychology is the strategies or tactics individuals take. Dark psychology includes control, misleading, and influence.

There are just 3% of people in the world who have mastered the ability of control. People accept that a great many people who choose to utilize dark psychology are the ones needing control. For one to be in charge, that means others must admire you and feel that you are in control. This strategy is, for the most part, utilized by individuals in power.

Since you have been born, you have consistently been a casualty of control by more powerful people, in any event, when you didn't understand it. Much the same as there are different sides of a coin, so are there different sides to psychology. A significant number of individuals are curious about one side, which is known as dark psychology. As the name suggests, it takes a look at the darkest deeds of individuals that exist. Another aspect right now is mind control. Everybody needs to control one another and everything else.

Let us imagine that you are an individual who has suffered much throughout everyday life. You suffered at school, you were mocked at work, or maybe you never succeeded in seduction. Do you realize that this can be changed essentially by studying at the very least the mental control applied to dark psychology?

If you don't have a clue on how to use mind control, don't worry, it's not your fault! You just have never been instructed because we are controlled by the TV and the news ... they are the ones who manipulate our minds!

Dark psychology is progressively growing among a lot of people all over the world. Therefore, it is significant for you to keep updated about its reality and mysteries behind dark psychology. The subjects and the ideas inside this book outfit you with the important information on understanding what extremely dark psychology is. This book will furnish you with the vital limit of having the option to avoid dark psychology at whatever point you are tempted to involve yourself in it. Later on, you will come to understand the benefits from when you read a book about dark psychology, which truly came to help you a great deal in managing matters concerning behavior and attitude.

1.

WHAT IS DARK PSYCHOLOGY?

Dark Psychology is the art and study of manipulation and brain control. While Psychology is the study of human behavior and is fundamental to our thinking, activities, and cooperation, the term Dark Psychology is the marvel by which people use strategies of inspiration, influence, control, and coercion to get what they need.

While dealing with my doctorate and considering abnormal psychology, I went over a term called "The Dark Triad" that refers to what numerous criminologists and psychologists pinpoint as a simple indicator of criminal behavior, just as risky, broken connections. The Dark Triad incorporates the attributes of ...

Dark Psychology Triad

Narcissism – Grandiosity, Egotism, and lack of sympathy.

Machiavellianism – Uses control to deceive and exploit people and has no feeling of deep quality.

Psychopathy – Often enchanting and friendly yet is described by impulsivity, self-centeredness, lack of sympathy, and callousness.

None of us need to be a victim of manipulation, yet it happens frequently. We may not be dependent upon somebody explicitly in the Dark Triad, yet typical, regular people like you and I face dark psychology strategies every day.

These strategies are frequently found in commercials, internet ads, sales techniques, and even our manager's behaviors. In case you have children (particularly young people), you will undoubtedly experience these strategies as your youngsters try different things with practices to get what they need and look for autonomy. Indeed, hidden control and dark persuasion are regularly utilized by people you trust and love. Here is a portion of the strategies routinely utilized by ordinary, regular people.

Love Flooding – Compliments, friendship or adulating somebody to make a request

Lying – Exaggeration, lies, fractional truths, untrue stories

Love Denial – Withhold attention and love

Withdrawal – Avoiding the individual or quiet treatment

Decision limitation – Giving specific decision alternatives that divert from the decision you don't need somebody to make

Reverse Psychology – Tell an individual a specific something or to do something with an expectation to spur them to do the opposite, which is truly what you want.

Semantic Manipulation – Using words that are expected to have a typical or mutual definition, yet the manipulator later reveals to you the individual in question has a different definition and understanding of the discussion.

The motivation behind this book isn't to disclose to you how to avoid being controlled and exploited (I'll expound on this in my next work). It's to help every one of us to remember that it is so natural to fall into utilizing these strategies so as to get what we need. I need to challenge you to assess your strategy in all everyday issues, including your work, administration, romantic relationships, parenting and friendship.

While a few people who use dark tactics know precisely what they are doing and they are deliberate about controlling you to get what they need, others utilize dark and untrustworthy strategies without being completely aware of it. A considerable amount of these people took in the strategy during youth from their parents. Others took in the strategy in their teenage years or adulthood unintentionally. They utilized a control strategy unexpectedly, and it worked. They got what they needed. In this manner, they keep on utilizing strategies that assist them in getting their way.

Now and again, people are prepared to utilize these strategies. Training programs that show dim, exploitative mental and persuasion tactics are regularly sales or marketing programs. A large number of these projects use dark strategy to make a brand or sell an item with the sole reason for serving themselves or their organization, not the client. A large number of these training programs persuade people that utilizing such strategies is alright and is to help the buyer. Since, obviously, their lives will be vastly improved when they buy the product or service.

Who utilizes Dark Psychology and manipulation tactics? Here's a rundown of people who appear to utilize these strategies the most.

Narcissists – People who are truly narcissistic (meeting clinical definitions) have a swelled feeling of self-worth. They need others to approve their belief of being superior. They have dreams of being loved and revered. They utilize dark psychology tactics, manipulation, and unethical persuasions to maintain this ideal.

Sociopaths – People who are genuinely sociopathic (meeting clinical standards), are regularly beguiling, intelligent, yet impulsive. Because of an absence of emotionality and capacity to feel regret, they utilize dark strategies to assemble a superficial relationship and then exploit people.

Lawyers – Some lawyers center so eagerly on winning their case that they resort to utilizing dark persuasion tactics to get the result they need.

Politicians – Some legislators utilize dark psychological tactics and dark persuasion tactics to persuade individuals they are correct and to get votes.

Salesmen – Many sales reps become so centered on achieving a deal that they utilize dark strategies to inspire and convince somebody to purchase their item.

Leaders – Some leaders utilize dark strategies to get consistency, more significant effort, or higher performance from their subordinates.

Public Speakers – Some speakers utilize dark strategies to increase the emotional condition of the crowd, realizing it leads to selling more items at the rear of the room.

Selfish People – This can be any individual who has a motivation of self before others. They will utilize strategies to address their issues first, even at another person's cost. They wouldn't fret win-lose results.

2.

WHAT IS NLP AND HOW IS IT DIFFERENT FROM DARK PSYCHOLOGY?

Neuro-linguistic programming is a method for changing somebody's thoughts and practices to help achieve desired outcomes for them.

The fame of neuro-linguistic programming or NLP has gotten across the board since it began during the 1970s. Its uses incorporated treatments of fears and tension issues and improvement of work environment performance or personal happiness.

NLP utilizes perceptual, behavioral, and communication procedures to make it simpler for individuals to change their thoughts and activities.

NLP depends on language processing; however ought not to be confused for regular language processing, which has the same acronym.

NLP was created by Richard Bandler and John Grinder, who trusted it was possible to identify the examples of thoughts and practices of effective people and to teach them to other people.

Regardless of the lack of empirical evidence to support it, Bandler and Grinder distributed two books, The Structure of Magic I and II, and NLP took off. Its popularity was mostly because of its adaptability in addressing the numerous various issues that people face.

How can it work?

The varying interpretations of NLP make it difficult to characterize. It is established on the possibility that people work by internal "maps" of the world that they learn through sensory experiences.
NLP tries to detect and modify oblivious inclinations or restrictions of a person's guide of the world.

NLP isn't hypnotherapy. Instead, it works through the conscious utilization of language to realize changes in somebody's thoughts and behavior.

For instance, a focal element of NLP is the possibility that an individual is one-sided towards one sensory framework, known as the preferred representational system or PRS.

Specialists can detect this preference through language. Expressions, for example, "I see your point," may flag a visual PRS. Or on the other hand, "I hear your point" may signal an auditory PRS.

An NLP specialist will recognize a people's PRS and base their helpful structure around it. The structure could include rapport-building, data social occasion, and objective setting with them.

Dark Side of Human Consciousness Concept

"Dark Psychology is both a human consciousness construct and study of the human condition as it identifies with the mental idea of individuals to go after others motivated by psychopathic, degenerate or psychopathological criminal drives that need a reason and general assumptions of instinctual drives, developmental science, and sociologies hypothesis. All of humankind can exploit people and other living animals. While many control or sublimate this tendency, some follow up on these driving forces. Dull Psychology investigates criminal, deviant, and cyber-criminal minds." Michael Nuccitelli, Psy.D. [2006]

Dark Psychology is the exploration of humanity as it correlates with the psychological tendency of some people to antagonize other people. All of humankind can victimize other humans & living creatures. While many limits or sublimate this tendency, some follow up on these driving forces. Dark Psychology looks to understand those considerations, perceptions, and feelings that lead to human predatory conduct. Dark Psychology expects that this creation is purposive and has some rational, goal-oriented motivation 99.99% of the time. The staying .01%, under Dark Psychology, is the ruthless exploitation of others without a purposive goal or sensibly characterized by evolutionary science or religious dogma.

Inside the following century, iPredators and their acts of theft, violence, and abuse will turn into a worldwide marvel and societal pandemic if not squashed. Portions of iPredators incorporate cyber stalkers, cyber terrorists, cybercriminals, online sexual predators, and political/religious fanatics occupied with digital warfare. Similarly, as Dark Psychology sees all criminal/deviant behavior on a continuum of seriousness and purposive aim, the hypothesis of iPredator follows a similar structure, yet includes abuse, assault, and online exploitation utilizing Information and Communications Technology. The meaning of iPredator is as per the following:

iPredator

iPredator: An individual, gathering, or country who, directly or indirectly, takes part in exploitation, victimization, coercion, stalking, theft, disparagement of others utilizing Information and Communications Technology [ICT]. iPredators are driven by deviant dreams, desires for power and control, requital, strict devotion, political reprisal, mental sickness, misperceptions, being accepted by those around you, or monetary or selfish gain. iPredators can be from any walk of life and are not defined by financial status, race, religion, or national heritage. iPredator is a global term used to recognize any individual who engages in criminal, coercive, deviant, or abusive behaviors utilizing ICT. Integral to the build is the reason that Information Age crooks, deviants, and the violently disturbed are psychopathological groupings new to humanity.

Regardless of whether the wrongdoer is a cyber-stalker, cyber harasser, cyber-criminal, online sexual stalker, cyber bully, internet troll, online child pornography consumer/distributor,cyber terrorist, or are engaged in web maligning or evil online deception, they fall inside the extent of iPredator. The three criteria used to characterize an iPredator include:

- A self-awareness of making hurt others, directly or indirectly, utilizing ICT.
- The use of ICT to get, trade, and deliver harmful data.
- A general understanding of Cyber-stealth used to take part in criminal or deviant activities or to profile, recognize, find, stalk, and connect with an objective.

Not at all like human predators before the Information Age, have iPredators depended upon the large number of advantages offered by Information and Communications Technology

[ICT]. These help incorporate trade of data over long separations, speed of data traded, and the boundless access to information accessible. Malignant in the plan, iPredators regularly mislead others utilizing ICT in theory and counterfeit the electronic universe known as the available. Like this, as the internet naturally offers all ICT clients anonymity, if they choose, iPredators effectively plan online profiles and diversionary strategies to stay undetected and untraceable.

Cyber-stealth, a sub-fundamental of iPredator, is a covert technique by which iPredators attempt to build up and continue total anonymity. At the same time, they take part in ICT exercises, arranging their next attack, examining creative reconnaissance advancements, or looking into the social profiles of their next objective. Simultaneous with the idea of Cyber-stealth is iPredator Victim Intuition [IVI], an iPredator's IVI is their inclination to detect an objective's ODDOR [Offline Distress Dictates Online Response], online and offline vulnerabilities, psychological weaknesses, technological limitations, expanding their success of a cyber-attack with minimal ramifications.

Arsonist

The Arsonist is an individual with an over obsessive preoccupation with fire setting. These people regularly have developmental histories loaded up with sexual and physical abuse. Usual among serial arsonists is the proclivity to be loners, have not many friends, and completely interested in fire and fire settings. Serial arsonists are profoundly ritualistic and will, in a general, display designed practices as to their techniques for setting fires.

Distracted by fire setting, Arsonists frequently fantasize and fixate upon how to design their fire setting episodes. When their objective is set on fire, a few arsonists experience sexual excitement and continue with masturbation while viewing. Despite their neurotic and formal examples, the serial arsonist feels pride in his activities.

Necrophilia

Thanatophilia, Necrophilia, and Necrologies all characterize a similar sort of maladjusted individual. There is a mental corruption which draws people to be attracted to corpses, and there are people who live with this disorder. The Diagnostic and Statistical Manual of Mental Disorders, by the American Psychiatric Association, defines necrophilia definitively as a paraphilia. A paraphilia is a biomedical term used to describe a person's sexual excitement and distraction with items, circumstances, or people that are not part of regularizing incitement and may cause trouble or significant issues for the individual. Consequently, a Necrophile's paraphilia is sexual excitement by an item, a deceased individual.

Specialists who have compiled profiles of Necrophiles show they have enormous difficulty experiencing a limit with regards to getting physically involved with others. For these individuals, sexual intimacy with the dead has a sense of security and security as opposed to sexual intimacy with a living human. Necrophiles have revealed in interviews feeling an incredible feeling of control when in the organization of a corpse. A sense of association gets optional to the essential requirement for perceived control.

Sequential Killer

A serial killer is a genuine human predator regularly characterized as somebody who murders at least three individuals over a time of 30 days or greater. Meetings with most serial killers have uncovered they experience a chilling period between each murder. The serial killer's chilling period is a perceptual refractory period whereby they are temporarily satisfied with their need to cause pain to others.

Criminal Psychology specialists have speculated their motivation for killing is the interest in an experience of psychological gratification just achieved using brutality. After the murder, these people feel a feeling of release joined with vain force. The experience for them brings such delight that they become wanton of feeling the experience of discharge and satisfaction by and by.

"The term 'serial killings' methods a progression of at least three killings, at the very least one of which was committed inside the United States, having normal qualities, for example, to recommend the sensible chance that the crimes were committed by a similar on-screen character or on-screen characters." FBI

3.

HOW OUR BODIES COMMUNICATE

On our NLP courses, you gain proficiency with the intensity of non-verbal communication in practical, hands-on training practices as opposed to only being told about it.

In these activities, people try different things with matching and then mis-coordinating their non-verbal behavior.

Also, the impact never ceases to amaze me.
It goes this way:

Martin and John conclude who is the 'matcher,' and then they talk about something important to them.

John, who is the matcher, quietly coordinates or copies Martin's non-verbal behavior for the first couple of minutes. He correlates Martin's eye to eye connection design, how they utilize their voice, and their overall posture.

At that point, John purposely and mismatched Martin's behavior. He looks away and starts looking about the room, or he talks in an altogether different voice example to Martin, or he makes some dramatic move in the act – at the same time carrying on the discussion in the very same manner.

There are no surprises

Keep in mind; there are no surprises. Every individual knows precisely what's going on and what will happen.

However, when the people in the 'Martin' job do the mismatching, there is perpetually a noticeable change in the 'John' person's behavior. They will by and large waver in their discussion, try to recover eye to eye contact, be not able to focus on what is being said, or will stop talking even though they maintain full awareness of their current circumstances.

What I find continually surprising, even though I have been utilizing the activity for a considerable length of time, is that the Martin-individual's response is not the slightest bit killed by the way that they KNOW it is only a setup exercise!

In talking about it a while later, individuals report that when they were first on the less than desirable finish of the mismatching behavior, they felt offended by the inconsistent, or felt stunned, or snubbed or felt as though the other individual had lost interest – even though they realized it was all essentially an exercise!

The power of non-verbal communication

Rationally they realize that it's only activity and that the mismatch isn't losing interest for them, nor are they deliberately insulting. In any case, emotionally, they react as though this is, to be sure, the mis-matcher's intention! Such is the power of non-verbal behavior!

The Mehrabian 7% Myth

The much-cited 'sacred goal' of communication skills' training is that our non-verbal behavior accounts for 93% of the effect of our message.

This depends on looking into what was done in 1967 by Albert Mehrabian and is, at any rate, a highly questionable 'certainty' that has been around for almost 50 years.

As indicated by this hypothesis, what you say accounts for a simple 7% of your effect when communicating eye to eye with somebody. The equation is as per the following:

55% of your effect is the outcome on how you show up

38% outcomes from how you sound

7% results from what you state!

So you can look great, smile a lot, articulate gobbledygook in a satisfying and significant way - and 93% of your message gets over...

The dubious formula is quoted, beyond a shadow of a doubt, in numerous books and a more significant part of communication skills' training programs.

It is certain that our non-verbal behavior is ground-breaking in fact – because it is to this non-verbal part of our communication that individuals most quickly and most emotionally respond.

Instincts and the Non-verbal

Nobody has yet come up with a thorough response to what precisely is intuition. But, it unquestionably incorporates the unconscious procedure of getting and handling non-verbal data.

This is going on always. Each move in an individual's feelings is transmitted to the world through their non-verbal - their body and voice.

At the point when you feel somewhat apprehensive, or relaxed, or irritated, or attracted, there are electrical and chemical changes all through your body: these influence blood stream and muscle tension.

Unconscious 'Leakage'

Because of this, there will be visible or audible alterations:

- In your eye, arm and leg developments.
- In the muscle tonus of your face and body.
- In your stance.
- In how you relax.
- In the beat in your neck.
- In the shade of your skin.
- In the size of your lips.
- In the constriction and dilation of your students.
- And in the sound and pace of your speech.

You may think you are working superbly at hiding your emotions, yet you are just concealing the gross and apparent signals.

There is as yet an unconscious 'leakage,' and this is usually gotten unconsciously by the other person. (Which just methods they are registering it without monitoring doing as such).

At some point or another (and this regularly happens after the experience is finished), this data that they have unconsciously gotten stands out enough to be noticed as a feeling about you – as an 'intuition.'

Why, it may very well be difficult to lie!

This is the reason- it is, in reality, extremely hard to be a good liar or con-artist. Our non-verbal will, for the most part, has let us down. A large portion of us have experienced the circumstance where you meet somebody and have a good conversation with them. Yet, subsequently, you have an uneasy feeling about them.

Normally you'll state something as "I don't have any idea... I can't exactly place it... however, I don't feel good about that person."

Ignore this at your peril!

We ignore our capacity to get non-verbal messages at our peril. Doing so is the reason for many a teenage broken heart (and many twenty-, forty-and sixty-year-old broken hearts, as well.)

You meet somebody, feel strongly attracted to them, and then start dating them. You energetically and productively ignore your intuition that they're not directly for you or are not to be trusted. And, sufficiently certain, your instinct proves directly at last. Furthermore, you're left to mourn the day your energy over-ran your intuition.

Non-Verbal Experts

Successful business-people tend not just to have a highly evolved natural receiving wire about individuals yet to also give conscious attention to it. Effective salesmen and serious sports-people, too.

Yet, the genuine specialists' right now to be – mothers!

With your mom lying is pointless. At any rate when you're up close and personal with her. You have a passing possibility on the phone since she's just got the voice to go on. In any case, it is difficult to convincingly lie to your mother face-to-face.

She has been finding a good pace non-verbal since numerous prior months you were even born!

NLP and Non-Verbal Communication

An inside and out NLP Course will try to guarantee that you gain a highly developed ability to perceive and react to this very subtle form of communication. This is because it is one of the foundation skills on which such a large amount of the NLP 'magic' depends. Applying NLP to communicate skilfully, or to develop/p extremely brilliant relationships, or do mentor somebody in self-improvement or to utilize the more significant part of the well-known NLP techniques necessitates that you have an excellent capacity to perceive non-verbal communication.

How to start?

1. Pick one region and stick with it for possibly 14 days – at that point, proceed onward to another. Maybe make the following scarcely any weeks your "Voice Tonality Period." Utilize this opportunity to truly hear voice tones. (This is a great place to start since you can also practice it on the phone.)

2. For the first 90 seconds (just) in any discussion, give the most attention to the tonality of the other person's voice. After 90 seconds, forget about it and carry on as usual.

3. At the day's end, abridge what you have found and perceived. Do this by chatting about your discoveries or review them in a notebook – or both. This is building up the ability to sharpen your senses – or, in NLP language, Sensory Acuity.

4. As you show signs of improvement at subtle shifts, moves in tonality start also to figure or, if fitting, get some information about what has changed in their mood. This is the building up of the skill of Calibrating – figuring out how to perceive what a specific move signals about the individual with whom you are conversing.

That is all you have to do. Following a long time of doing this, your Sensory Acuity and capacity to calibrate right now have improved significantly. Presently proceed onward to another area. You could start to study the connection between state, breathing examples, and mood shifts.

Words of caution and encouragement

It's anything but a smart thought to show off your recently developed skill as a kind of gathering piece or an 'I can read your mind' trick.

People are susceptible to how you react to their non-verbal communication. Showing a lack of respect for it might well make long-term animosity.

On the other hand, perceiving and reacting consciously and appropriately to non-verbal communication is one of the best methods for creating and looking after compatibility.

For whatever length of time that you do cause a person's conscious attention to what you are doing or what you have done, your skill right now improves your capacity to make and to keep up suffering individual, social, and professional relationships.

4.

THE 23 POWERFUL TECHNIQUES FOR PERSUADING AND INFLUENCING PEOPLE WITH MENTAL MANIPULATION AND NLP

Technique 1: How to lie

Disordered characters sometimes lie, however some of the time lie in any event when there is no obvious or helpful purpose for the lying. They are additionally expert at lying in a wide variety of ways, some of which are quite subtle.

For the disordered character, lying fills some needs. In any case, mainly, lying serves to give a controller an advantage over someone else. Disordered characters don't need you to realize what they're about or what they're doing. That would make even the odds in your experiences with them. However, upset characters need to be one-up on you and a step ahead of you. They need to keep you out of the loop and keep you speculating. Probably the ideal approach to do this is by deception.

Disordered characters are genuinely educated about even the most subtle and stealthy approaches to lie

There are such a significant number of approaches to lie that it's practically difficult to show them all. But disordered characters are truly proficient about even the most subtle and stealthy methods to lie and are artful in their utilization of the different types of lying.

One subtle way to deal with lying will be lying by omission. At the point when somebody needs to deceive you, they don't need to make an obviously absurd or bogus case. Ordinarily, they should simply ensure they don't inform every bit of relevant information regarding something. It's as simple as leaving out a significant detail or something vital to gleaning an understanding of the whole situation. A example of an aging salesman concerned about his professional stability who asked as to whether there were any designs to lay him off or fire him. His supervisor let him know there were no such plans. But, he didn't reveal to him that his business accounts were going to be shared with a new, younger employee and that before long, he'd be in a situation wherein he may incline toward early retirement instead of decreasing commissions. Once in a while, what a person doesn't state or do can be a substantially more powerful manipulation tool.

Another kind of subtle lying is the utilization of vagueness. At the point when you face a manipulator about an issue, they may offer you a response, yet they may also be so vague about the details that you wind up remaining to a great extent in the dark. Once in a while, the disordered character can control you adequately by doing just the opposite. By utilizing specificity in a reaction so that it might give a limited response to the question you've asked, however, without giving extra detail, that would better address the intent of your question.

Lying by distortion of crucial details gives one other approach to darken the master plan and deceive somebody. Indeed, when somebody truly needs to lie effectively, they'll frequently recite a litany of facts (all to give the feeling that they're on a fact telling binge) while at the same time forgetting about a critical few details or bending the truth of an important fact.

Lying is such an ingrained habit for people with these disorders that occasionally, they end up midway accepting their lies. That is genuine for the lies they tell others, yet additionally, for the lies they let themselves know.

By lying so regularly about the truth of situations, the upset character blocks and resists any opportunity that they will disguise the most fundamental standards of responsible conduct.

Technique 2: How to tell a story

"Manipulation is a sincerely unhealthy psychological strategy utilized by individuals who are a psychological strategy for requesting what they need and need directly," says Sharie Stines, a California-based advisor who has practical experience in abuse and toxic relationships. "Individuals who are trying to manipulate others are attempting to control others."

There are various types of control, going from a pushy sales rep to an emotionally abusive partner— and a few practices are simpler to spot than others.

Here, specialists clarify the indications that you could be the subject of control. You feel fear, obligation, and guilt

Manipulative behavior includes three elements, as indicated by Stines: fear, obligation, and guilt. "At the point when somebody is controlling you, you are in effect mentally forced into doing something you likely would prefer truly not to do," she says. You may feel scared to do it, committed to doing it, or guilty about not doing it.

She focuses on two basic manipulators: "the bully" and "the person in question." A bully practices methods which keep you fearful and may utilize hostility, threats, and intimidation to control you, she says. The victim incites a feeling of blame in their objective. "The victim typically acts hurt," Stine says. Yet, while the manipulator frequently plays the person in question, actually they are the ones who have caused the issue, she includes.

An individual who is targeted by manipulators who play the unfortunate casualty regularly try to help the manipulator to quit feeling guilty, Stines says.

Focuses on this sort of control frequently feel answerable for helping the victim by doing whatever they can to stop their suffering.

You're questioning yourself

The term "gaslighting" is frequently used to recognize control that gets individuals to question themselves, their existence, memory, or thoughts. A manipulative person may wind what you state and make it about them, hijack the discussion or cause you to feel as you've done something incorrectly when you're not exactly sure you have, as indicated by Stines

In case you're being gaslighted, you may feel a false feeling of blame or defensiveness—like you totally flopped or probably did something wrong when truly that is not the situation, as per Stines.

"Manipulators blame," she says. "They don't assume liability."

Wow, shocking.

"In case some help isn't achieved for you since at that point it isn't 'for the sake of entertainment and nothing,'" says Stines. "If there are surprises, at that point, control is happening."

Stines refers to one sort of controller as 'Mr. Decent Guy.' This person may be useful and do a lot of favors for others. "It is exceptionally confusing because you don't understand anything negative is going on," she says. "But, then again, with each great deed, there is a string attached—an expectation." If you don't meet the manipulator's desire, you will be described as unreasonable, Stines says.

Exploiting the standards and desires for interchange is one of the most widely recognized types of manipulation, says Jay Olson, a doctoral specialist examining control at McGill University.

A salesperson, for instance, may cause it to appear because the individual gave you an arrangement, you should purchase the item. In a relationship, a partner may get you to open up, and at that point demand something in return. "These strategies work since they misuse social standards," says Olson. "It's entirely expected to respond favorably, however in any event, when somebody does one deviously, we regularly still feel compelled to respond and agree."

Get the most recent career, relationship, and well-being advice to improve your life: pursue TIME's Living bulletin.

You notice the 'foot-in-the-door' and 'door in-the-face' strategies

Frequently, manipulators attempt one of two strategies, says Olson. The first is the foot-in-the-door method, where somebody begins with a little and sensible request—like, do you have the opportunity?— which at that point leads into a more significant request—like I need $10 for a taxi. "This is regularly utilized in road scams," Olson says.

"The door in-the-face strategy is the inverse—it includes somebody making a big request, having it dismissed, at that point making a smaller one," Olson clarifies.

"Somebody doing contract work, for instance, may approach you for a huge total of cash in advance, and then after you decay, will request a smaller sum. This works since, following the larger request, the smaller appeal appears to be sensible." States Olson.

Technique 3: Voice control

Research has indicated that people frequently apply command over their feelings. By modulating expressions, reappraising feelings, and diverting consideration, they can manage their emotional experience. These discoveries have added to an obscuring of the conventional limits among intellectual and emotional procedures, and it has been proposed that emotional signs are created in an objective, coordinated manner and checked for mistakes like other deliberate activities. In any case, this exciting chance has never been experimentally tried. To this end, we made an advanced sound stage to covertly modify the emotional tone of members' voices while they talked toward satisfaction, misery, or fear. The outcome indicated that the sound changes were being seen as regular instances of the familiar feelings, however the extraordinary larger part of the members, all things considered, stayed unaware that their own voices were being manipulated. This finding shows that individuals are not constantly observing their voice to ensure that it meets a predetermined emotional target. Instead, as an outcome of tuning in to their modified voices, the emotional condition of the members changed in congruence with the emotion portrayed, which was estimated by both self-report and skin conductance level. This change is the first proof, as far as anyone is concerned, of peripheral feedback effects for emotional involvement with the sound-related area. Our outcome reinforces the more extensive structure of self-observation hypothesis: that we regularly utilize the same inferential strategies to understand ourselves from those that we use to get others.

Technique 4: Eye contact

General Principles for Making Effective Eye Contact

Eye to eye connection sires eye to eye contact. You may be reluctant to look at people since you would prefer to think them not to look at you. And, sufficiently certain, when you take a look at them the first time when they turn away. In any case, they're likely turning away because they're figuring something very similar you did; that you would prefer truly not to look at them! Even if you've made the initial move, they're still worried about rejection. Yet, the vast majority are simply trusting that consent will get into a shared look. Studies have demonstrated that once one individual in a chatting pair starts a more noteworthy eye to eye contact, the other individual will take action accordingly and increase their degree of eye to eye contact also.

But don't be a creeper. Altogether, for the eye to eye contact to be powerful, it should be welcome and proper. At the point when eye to eye contact is unwanted, it goes from looking to staring, and being stared at makes people uncomfortable. Eye contact brings about physiologic arousal—it increments the prefrontal mind action and activates the thoughtful sensory system, speeding up an individual's pulse, sweat, and relaxing. What's more, this happens not just when you're simply investigating somebody's eyes, yet additionally when you see that somebody is staring at you. This excitement can be something worth being thankful for if you and a beautiful woman are investigating each other's eyes; it can make a more extraordinary connection. But, when somebody fixes their look on you in an offensive manner, it can feel as though a predator is stalking you in the wild; it sets off your threat-meter.

Subsequently, great eye to eye connection depends on mutuality. As Michael Ellsberg, creator of The Power of Eye Contact puts it:

"All together for the eye to eye connection to feel better, one individual can't force his visual will on another; it is a shared experience. Maybe eyes meet just for a second from the start; one partner at that point tries things out and tries a couple of moments, and when that is met energetically, the pair can start to increase the eye to eye connection together until they are secured by a delightful move of eyes and looks." [Emphasis mine]

After you've made two attempts to start eye to eye connection with somebody, if they don't respond by any means, give it up.

At the point when you're with somebody you're not as familiar with, recline as you increment your eye to eye connection. The bit of included space between you adjust the more significant eye to eye connection you're making, allowing the receiver of your look to feel more comfortable and keeping the closeness level from ramping up too quickly. On the other hand, when somebody is talking with you about something exceptional and individual, fit in as you maintain eye contact with them to show that you're giving them your full attention.

Focus on each eye in turn and switch between them. At the point when you're sitting near somebody, you can't take a look at both of their eyes simultaneously, and if you try to, your look will become off-putting and laser-like. You may have never halted to consider it, yet when you look at somebody without flinching, it is simply their eye; you take a look at each of their eyes in turn. You are most likely as of now have one eye (the left or the right) that you will, in general, focus on. However, it's acceptable to change your look from one eye to the next during a discussion (it's very common and shows more attention and interest). Try not to dance your look between their eyes too much of the time—you would prefer not to show up as though you're watching a Ping-Pong match. Easily and normally.

A few people recommend that since you can't glance in both of a person's eyes simultaneously, you should simply gaze at the bridge of their nose. Yet, people can once in a while tell you're doing that, causing the strategy to appear to be fake and even manipulative.

Try not to try too hard. More eye to eye connection is acceptable... to a limited extent. You would prefer not to stare at somebody for a whole discussion. About at regular intervals, or about the time it takes to talk a single sentence, turn away from their eyes for a second or so and then turn back once more. Locate a natural rhythm. Don't include the seconds in your mind.

If you feel lost concerning how to find that musicality from the start, try the "triangle technique." Look at one of the individual's eyes for a beat, at that point the other eye for a beat, at that point at their mouth, and then back at their first eye. Repeat. As you practice this technique and understand what great eye to eye connection feels like, you ought to have the option to discard the set example for a stream that falls into place without any issues.

It's fine to turn away from somebody when you're trying to gather your thoughts.

Also note that it's very ordinary and proper to look away and turn away from somebody as you review a memory, ponder something over, or gather your thoughts about what you need to say next.

At the point when you break your look, look to the side, not down—looking down when you break somebody's look signals lower-status, disgrace, or potential submission. Not the sort of message you need to pass on. Rather, break your look on a level plane.

Work your way up. Improving your eye to eye connection is something you can do moderately quickly and no problem at all. It just takes practice. Begin by expanding your eye to eye connection with your family; you may find you don't look at your sibling in the eye when you talk with him. At that point, increase your eye to eye connection with your friends, and then your associates. As you begin to feel greater, maintaining eye contact with people, take a shot at looking at salespeople and servers. At long last, begin looking at outsiders and new people you meet. In a little while, you'll be a genuine eye to eye contact specialist!

Tips for Eye Contact in Specific Circumstances:

In the Salesforce or on Business calls

When criticizing or giving feedback to an employee: Sitting directly up close and personal causes the discussion to appear to be additionally scary and cross-examination like. Rather, sit opposite the worker at around a 45-degree edge, with the hand you're writing with nearest to the employee. This calculated position makes it more regular for you to sway your look between the employee's eyes and the desk work before you.

When trying to make a sale: In case you're a salesman, looking at potential buyers is significant in building trust and rapport, but on the other hand, it's helpful to look for when they look at you. They'll regularly do that when you've said something that particularly interests them, so delay and develop that point or product feature.

At the point when you're making a pitch: Look at everybody in the room. Try not to look at the president yet, not the veep. Remember to look at the secretary as well.

In a job interview: In a prospective employee meeting, eye to eye connection is second in significance possibly to dress with regards to non-verbal influencers. One examination found that questioners "were bound to contract and rate as valid and appealing interviewees who kept up an ordinary or high level of look than the people who deflected their look." So make certain to make great, strong eye to eye connection with the questioner utilizing the tips above.

When You Want to Intimidate

Look when you talk than when you tune in. People who have a higher-status look when they're talking, and less eye to eye connection when they're tuning in; this shows power. Those with lower-status do the inverse, and this shows power. A high proportion of addressing listening eye to eye connection is referred to as visual dominance.

Presently remember that in many associations, regardless of whether you do have higher-status than the individual with whom you're conversing, the ideal approach is to reach whether you're talking or tuning in. It pays to reach when listening, as it causes the other person to feel significant, and causing others to feel significant is the key part of getting enchanting and along these lines powerful. Broadly alluring men like Ronald Reagan and Bill Clinton were notable for their capacity to cause every individual they met to feel like nobody else in the room made a difference, and they did that by staring at the individual and truly listening to him or her.

In any case, in circumstances where it is favorable to show that there's a pecking order and that you're on it, have a go at looking when you talk and less when you tune in.

Hide your eyes. At the point when somebody covers his eyes, the communication and input among him and someone else becomes one-sided. The "eye-less" fellow can perceive what's new with the other individual, yet the other person doesn't have the foggiest idea about what's new with the eye-less person. This is the reason contemplates have demonstrated that the individuals who spread their eyes appear to be all the more remarkable and in charge—even though this imbalance also normally makes hatred from those they interact with. This is the reason cops in reflected shades can appear to be threatening, why individuals who wear shades inside tick others off, and why Darth Vader is so darn scary.

Stare them down. At the point when you can't or don't have any desire to cover your eyes, yet you, despite everything, need to scare somebody, it's just an issue of gazing them down and not being the person who turns away first. The individual who keeps up his look shows predominance and higher-status, while the individual who turns away first signals their submission. Keeping up your glare shows that you're sure, which can, in some cases, assist mind with excursion an adversary or convince the person who needs to battle you at the restaurant to move on.

Martial Artists have mastered the stare-down:
Making Eye Contact with a Stranger on the Street

To start with, for what reason would you need to do this at any rate? Well, Michael Ellsberg argues that creative eye to eye connection with strangers you pass on the road isn't just excellent practice for looking at individuals you know, and can lead to getting more dates, it can even "change the urban landscape:"

"Before I began doing this, I would walk around the city, and for the most part, see the others I experienced as obstacles or annoyances. But when I began doing it—when I began investigating the windows of many individuals' souls every day—the entire scene moved. I out of nowhere observed such a great amount of excellence out there, so much pity. Such a significant number of substantial weights, so much euphoria... The city turned into an ensemble of feeling—all from this basic move."

According to Ellsberg, there are a couple of keys to effectively looking at strangers in the city, and they fundamentally all rotate around the way that you don't need your eye to eye connection to cause people to feel threatened. To begin with, he suggests keeping your outward appearance unbiased and your look delicate—the eye and face muscles are loose, no laser-eyes. Second, you would prefer not to start eye to eye connection with somebody from excessively far away; you should attempt to look at the individual when you're around 4-5 paces from running into each other. At last, just investigate their eyes for a speedy minute—around one pace or sufficiently long to see their eye color.

When Talking to Other Men

As we referenced before, eye contact makes physical and mental arousal, expanding action in the recipient's prefrontal brain and accelerating their breathing and pulse. For men, this physiological reaction can cause a high-stakes discussion to feel too confrontational. So when you need to talk with another man about something significant, do it one next to the other—go for a drive, or a walk, or fishing together.

When Trying to Woo Women

Eye contact is perhaps the ideal methods for building attraction with the women and is gainful in each phase of a relationship:

The Initial Encounter

Looking at a lady. While you may think about your degree of engaging quality as unchangeable, studies have demonstrated that how appealing you look to others is impacted by things like your facial expression, and, you got it, regardless of whether you're looking toward them. Taking a look at a lady directly, while additionally grinning, causes you to show up more appealing to her. The most appealing face to show a lady is unified with a direct eye to eye connection, a casual face (don't show pressure, particularly in your jaw), and an easy smile.

If a lady meets your eyes, don't be the first to turn away. Keep in mind, the person who holds the look longer shows power; you're not trying to assert your predominance here—maintaining eye contact with you mainly flags your certainty, which is appealing to ladies.

- Interpreting her eye to eye connection. At the point when you talk with a lady, she will typically turn away, regardless of whether she's keen on you or not. But, how she deflects her look discloses to you a great deal about whether she needs you to move toward her or not:

- If she looks back at you after looking down in 45 seconds after the fact, she is almost definitely interested. This sign is so about flat fall verification that you needn't bother with any smooth pick-up lines when you approach her—simply offer your hand and present yourself.

• If she turns away on a level plane, she doesn't know whether she's keen on you or not yet. Grin and look again to perceive how she responds.

• If she turns away her look by looking into, she's not interested. Fundamentally, she simply rolled her eyes at you.

After You Meet

When you've gotten a woman's attention, and have begun conversing with her, don't ease up on the eye to eye connection, since it will keep on receiving rewards. In our past article, we discussed how eye to eye connection cultivates close bonds, and that is a help in case you're trying to prevail upon a lady.

In an investigation directed by Dr. Arthur Aron, outsiders were brought into a lab and combined off into other gender couples. The recently shaped couples who were approached to investigate each other's eyes for two minutes in a row later announced feelings of attraction, love, and even love for their partners. One of the couples even proceeded to wed.

Once You've Been Together Awhile

So eye to eye connection can help start a relationship and then develop its power. In long term relationships it can even help keep feelings of love alive. Studies have indicated that couples with the most grounded love for one another additionally look and hold common looks for longer time-frames. Presently connection isn't causation—does looking at one another more keep you in love, or is it simply that the individuals who are in love need to take a gander at one another all the more frequently? Most likely, a greater amount of the last mentioned. However, it absolutely couldn't damage to try to "find" (in the Avatar sense, normally) your partner all the more regularly. Make some goo-goo eyes over supper every once in a while.

When Giving a Speech

Speakers who look at the crowd are seen as more trustworthy, competent, and confident. Eye to eye connection additionally causes you to construct a more prominent feeling of closeness among you and your crowd, and this association makes ethos, which thus makes your message all the more convincing. Somebody who's continually taking a look at their notes appears to be anxious (Do they have something to cover up? Are they not capable enough to get ready sufficiently?) And is bound to be rejected.

At the point when you're addressing a large audience, it is impractical to look at every single individual in participation. A few people will instruct you to counterfeit it by investigating everybody's heads—except you won't persuade anybody with that technique. You additionally shouldn't do the head bobber thing where you take a look at your notes for a second and then rapidly at your crowd and then back at your notes... Finally, don't "spray" your look over the crowd like you're shooting it from an aerosol can. Rather, you need to look at singular individuals from the audience.

To have the option to do this, you first need to try to retain your speech, and if you can't do that completely, at that point, make a layout with simply your primary concerns, so you just need to look down a couple of times to discover your direction.

Since your eyes are allowed to meander around the room, you can approach looking at people in the crowd in a couple of various ways, contingent upon the size of the crowd:

30 individuals or less: At the point when you're tending to a little gathering, state around a meeting table, don't continue moving your look clockwise or counterclockwise around the table, halting to make a couple of moments of the eye to eye connection with every individual before clearing around once more. Individuals will start to foresee and kind of fear their "turn." Always be seeing somebody, however, keep who you take a look at random and blend it up all through your presentation.at at least 30 individuals. Try the triangle technique; it's a lot like the triangle strategy for up close and personal associations referenced above, just with entire people swapped for the person's eyes and mouth.

Imagine an invisible triangle sitting on the crowd. You look at an individual on the correct side purpose of the triangle, and then the top point, and then the left point. At that point, practice. To blend it up and shield your example from getting unsurprising, you invert the triangle every once in a while.

75-300 individuals: Partition the audience into five non-existent groups, and then move your look from group to group, picking an alternate individual inside the gathering to look at each time.

300+ people: If it's a huge crowd, at that point, center your eye to eye connection on individuals in the first not many columns while also watching out into the group now and then.

With any of these techniques, the key is to move your look from individual to individual coolly and easily. You don't need it to appear to be jerky... "You there! Feel the presence of my eyes! Also, you! And you!"

Three last tips for talks, paying little mind to crowd size:

Open with an eye to eye connection. At the point when you find a workable place to speak from, usually the front of the room, take a couple of seconds to grin and look at people before you even start talking. This is a great way to start off on the right foot.

Try not to keep your eyes stuck on the Powerpoint slides. To start with, you should accept the advice of Alex Hunter and keep your slides incredibly basic and clean. And, second, you ought to be very acquainted with what's on each slide, so you don't need to continue taking a look at them and exhausting the jeans off individuals by reading the slides to them.

Take a look at both friendly faces and hostile faces. Don't simply look at the well friendly faces in the group. Take a gander at the threatening, exhausted faces as well. Looking at them could mollify them a little for your message. Yet, in the wake of taking a look at a hostile face for somewhat, at that point, take a look at the individuals who are radiating up at you to shield your energy from hailing.

Remember to look at individuals toward the finish of the discourse. It's anything but difficult to become involved with racing to complete. However, the crescendo is the point at which you truly need to leave an effect. Make sure to investigate individuals' eyes as you near truly drive your message home.

Technique 5: Use a positive mood

State of mind deep affects how individuals see their general surroundings. Throughout the years, the state of mind has appeared to influence memory forms, judgment and dynamics, and influence. Temperament also influences the procedures individuals use when preparing approaching data. When all is said in done, positive dispositions seem to advance worldwide, adaptable, natural, and holistic information processing (see Isen 1999, 2004 for outlines). Negative mindsets, interestingly, have been related to more precise, restricted, centered, and investigative types of preparation (see Schwarz and Clore 1996 for an audit).

Mind-set doesn't, in any case, produce predictable primary impacts on data processing. Despite what might be expected, the impacts of state of mind seem adaptable and setting subordinate. For example, the impacts of mind-set might be directed by the individual understanding of its implications, and by situational requests. Moreover, the impacts of state of mind on data preparation seem to fluctuate with message valence. As per the indulgent possibility perspective on temperament, individuals by and large endeavor to keep up, or achieve positive disposition states. In constructive disposition states, individuals are well on the way to take care of data that is indulgently fulfilling, for example, messages that contain elevating and positive data and most drastically unwilling to take care of messages that may ruin a positive state of mind. A positive state of mind is accordingly proposed to incite deliberate preparing of uplifting messages, and heuristic handling of aversive, unpleasant messages. When feeling negative, data preparation will be significantly less dependent upon the decadent results of a message, basically because negative states of mind are bound to improve paying little mind to message content. All in all, exact examinations have supported libertine possibility suppositions.

In any case, recent findings propose that a positive state of mind may advance the efficient handling of negative data when the data is pertinent to oneself. From the start, these discoveries show up inconsistent with libertine possibility suspicions. There is a minimal indulgent award in facing negative or in any event, undermining realities about oneself. These findings in this manner recommend that there are cases where a positive mindset doesn't advance a decadent quest for joy yet rather adjusts people to 'face up to the realities.' In the following segment, we talk about this specific capacity of mind-set and the directing job of self-significance in more detail.

Mood and self-threatening information

Individuals are commonly hesitant to face unpleasant, self-important realities. For example, individuals will, in general, make light of negative input about their characters by conjuring up reasons that undermine the exactness of the feedback. Also, beneficiaries of undermining well-being messages regularly trivialize the individual pertinence of the data, limit the reality of a well-being risk, or participate in wishful thinking. From a self-guideline point of view, such reactions serve a significant capacity: they secure a person against negative emotions such as fear, anxiety, and depression, and help to keep up a constructive mental self-view. By the by, not acknowledging the clear issues can be an issue, especially in the well-being domain, where powerful messages are intended to prevent illness. Hence, recent examination efforts have concentrated on methodologies that make people all the more accepting of aversive yet self-significant data.

One procedure that seems to build acknowledgment of self-threatening data is the acceptance of a positive state of mind. In particular, a positive state of mind may build relative interest in negative feedback about oneself, in this way constricting a worldwide inclination for the positive feedback.

Also, a positive mind-set expanded interest for feedback about individual weakness just when the data was pertinent to a self-related objective. Of specific importance to the present examination, the acceptance of a positive state of mind upgraded influence in regards to a message that depicted the hurtful impacts of caffeine consumption just when the data was significant to oneself, for example, just for caffeine purchasers. At the point when the data was not significant to oneself, a positive state of mind had no impact on influence. Concerning data handling, the impacts of a positive state of mind may also be directed without anyone else's importance.

At the point when an aversive message is irrelevant to the self, precise message handling has personal expenses, since it ruins a positive state of mind, and no close to home advantages, because there are no suggestions for oneself. Appropriately, a positive state of mind is probably going to actuate a quest for indulgent concerns and advance less systematic methods of data processing. For messages with high significance to oneself, concentrated message handling will involve transient full of feeling costs, yet also, advantage the self in the more drawn out run, for example, by obtaining significant data that may help improve a significant self-idea. In these conditions, a positive state of mind is probably going to advance methodical message processing. To put it plainly, ongoing exploration proposes that people may, at times, utilize a constructive state of mind as an asset to "survive" the transient, full of feeling expenses of efficient training, possibly undermining data, to get longer-term advantages of the data for oneself. The specific elements of this procedure, but, have not yet been efficiently tended to.

More specifically, strong proof concerning the intuitive impacts of self-importance and disposition on data preparation has stayed lacking. As indicated by double procedure models of influence, a far-reaching and strong trial of data preparation would require impacts of the nature of the contentions in an enticing message on two kinds of ward measures. In particular, efficient processing is induced if members separate among strong and weak arguments on attitudes toward an influential message. As it were, members who process a message efficiently ought to concur more with this message to the degree that it contains strong arguments, rather than weak arguments. Furthermore, efficient message handling shows itself by the degree and valence of issue-significant thoughts recipients create in light of the message, with the end goal that recipients ought to produce more thoughts steady of message content, and fewer thoughts limiting message content, to the degree that a message contains strong arguments, as opposed to weak arguments.

So far, communications between self-relevance, mind-set, and argument quality on musings and perspectives toward a threatening message have not been tried observationally. Also, separate from the proposed impacts of state of mind on controlled, efficient processing, it is unclear whether the impacts of temperament additionally stretch out to more automatic, understood types of data preparation. Recent studies suggest that a positive mind-set elevates access to certain, intuitive information on what is significant to oneself, as far as general objectives, motives, and experiences, and adjusts people to 'the fantastic plan of things.' A positive mindset may hence elevate access to understood, instinctive assets expected to pass judgment on the self-pertinence of approaching data, and, if important, switch preparing mode. In any case, the understood procedures engaged with the impacts of temperament on the acknowledgment of self-undermining data have received little empirical attention.

The key goal of the present research is in this manner to expand previous findings by giving a hearty observational trial of the subjective procedures engaged with the impacts of temperament on the acknowledgment of threatening health information in two explicit manners. To begin with, the present examination gives an express trial of the intelligent impacts of self-significance, temperament, and argument quality on subjective procedures and influence. Second, the present research extends past discoveries by testing understood reactions to self-compromising versus non-undermining data. The central theory that we set forward is that a positive state of mind will advance both controlled, systematic processing of self-compromising health information, just as automatic, verifiable participation to self-threatening information.

Technique 6: Ask the right Questions and Listen

Is it just me, or do individuals break down their discussions once they are done? You know, experiencing it again at the top of the priority list, considering better words that could have passed on what they needed in a superior manner? After the individual has proceeded onward, it's simply me overthinking what I just said to them, like practically everything else, editing, proofing, until it turns into this ideal duplicate fit to be delivered. In any case, yes, there's a trick, genuine discussions don't occur that way, isn't that right? They're spontaneous. Which is both energizing and, well, for the individuals who are timid as am I, intimidating. Imagine being frightened by something as rudimentary as starting a discussion. Fearing what comes so normally to everyone around me (I'm expecting here). How would you get a message over, or, in worst-case scenarios, how would you recognize what you feel since you can't discuss viably with even yourself!

The beneficial thing here is people are ever developing. They aren't meant to be stale in one place or condition. They try to improve to lead the existence they need and deserve! Furthermore, that is the thing that I strive to do, as well. Consistently. I wouldn't fret requesting help from the people who are acceptable at what I 'need,' yet a great deal of times, these 'suggestions' and 'motivational talks' have me no place.

I ran over a quickened learning methodology for the recognition and use of examples on the planet: Neuro-Linguistic Programming (NLP) – neuro from nervous system science; linguistic(s) for language; and programming refers to how the arrangement of nervous system science and language works in our brain. This appeared to be acceptable, practically like I would get familiar with the language of my mind! Much the same as each new field, NLP training and coaching is as yet a developing field in Pakistan, despite having begun during the 80s in the west. Just now, people in Pakistan are inclined towards picking up/knowing brain sciences; some may be more interested in putting resources into themselves, their own psychological and mental growth. Since it's costly, you would prefer not to go ignorant. Arslan Larik, Certified Master Coach and Trainer by the American Board of Neuro-Linguistic Programming (NLP), Timeline Therapy, Hypnosis, and ICF, and an emotional entrepreneur with a strong belief in the power of empathy, breaks it down for Us.

Clearing misconceptions

Before we understand what NLP is, we should investigate what it's most certainly not.

#1: NLP is manipulative and is a form of mind control.

Reality: I haven't seen anybody control another person utilizing NLP even though you can utilize NLP to impact others. More often than not, individuals can't control themselves.

NLP can empower you to get into compatibility with others and their unconscious mind, and then you can expand your capacity to affect and impact them. The more you can interface with somebody unconsciously, the more you will have the option to impact them. I was instructing at an NLP training once, and I had this realtor, Y, who was interested in bringing more deals to a close. I had Y show me the process he used when demonstrating open houses to prospective buyers. I honestly had some moments of clarity as I understood he was not interfacing enough to his prospects' feelings. By making some minor changes to his business procedure by utilizing NLP methods, the preparation was more successful. That wouldn't mind control; NLP is tied in with associating with people at an emotional or oblivious level outside of their conscious awareness.

#2: NLP doesn't or won't work for me

Reality: I realize that a few people who have studied or experienced NLP have had an experience of attempting a method and not getting the outcome they needed. One of the key abilities of NLP is having the option to tailor your activities and practices. We call this "behavioral flexibility." This means you need to watch, watch and listen for clues that mention to you what's happening for you or for the people you are trying to impact. When you utilize your perceptual or sensory abilities, you can change your methodology as needs be. You are most likely previously getting incredible outcomes in a few or numerous aspects of your life. You are utilizing approaches and methods you may not know about that are working well for you. NLP causes you to nurture a better understanding of how things influence you and those you are in contact with and how to make them function even better. And, if there are regions that are not working well for you regularly, rolling out minor improvements to a procedure or system is exactly what you have to have a major effect on your own, or your professional, results.

What is NLP?

At the point when NLP was first developed, the early models fundamentally cited people getting incredible outcomes working in the field of treatment. In any case, along the way, many of the behaviors, abilities, and methods happened to be incredibly helpful in different settings, including communication, impact, and change. I have seen NLP utilized effectively with regards to authority, sports, deals and influence, open talking, and customized one-on-one instruction to give some examples.

I've also watched newly-trained NLP students consistently assist individuals with beating habits or constraining beliefs in a single meeting. But, it doesn't make them an advisor. Individuals can increase restorative advantages from numerous things, such as reading a book, taking some time off, walking amid nature, and reflecting. That doesn't make its treatment.

What considers successful therapy is when individuals who work intimately with mentors and specialists in one-on-one sessions in the wake of having collapsed or snapped mentally, can overcome obstacles and achieve performance and behavioral transformation. Each excellent minute, be it an individual effort or a couple struggling to keep their marriage, has driven me to gain proficiency with a ton about human examples and how our brain capacities.

Preparing your mind

In circumstances such as these, when we are under lots of pressure, negative thoughts come naturally. It's a sure reasoning that you need to make a conscious effort about. One approach to teaching it as a propensity is to practice appreciation. Get it done each day, similar to an activity, such as going through an hour at a gym.

A business master and a phenomenal coach in the course of his life, Zig Zagler, was gone up against by a young lady at one of his workshops who needed to change her point of view. As indicated by her, everyone at her office was planning against her. He asked her to think of things that were certain in her work environment and to write them down in her journal. Things like "I have access to clean drinking water at the office" are typically underestimated. There's no damage in pointing higher; simply don't forget to count your blessings. At the point when you have a list, remain before a mirror and rehash them consistently – noisy and clear, with energy (mantra). "I love my activity in light of the fact that –." A month later he followed up with her, and her point of view had definitely changed.

At that point comes forgiveness. It's the hardest of all, regardless of whether you "state" you have forgiven the individual who has hurt you in any capacity. The test of forgiveness in any religious practice is the point at which you can petition God for that individual.

Technique 7: Keep attention on the interests of the other person

Hear What People Are Saying

Listening is one of the most significant skills you can have. How well you listen majorly affects your job effectiveness, and on the nature of your associations with others.
For example:

- We tune in to get data.

- We tune in to understand.
- We tune in for satisfaction.
- We tune in to learn.

You'd think we'd be masters at listening, what with all of it that we do every day! Indeed, the vast majority of us are not, and studies propose that we only retain between 25 and 50 percent of what we hear, as depicted by Edgar Dale's Cone of Experience. That means that when you converse with your chief, partners, clients, or life partner for 10 minutes, they focus on not precisely 50% of the discussion.

If you flip it over to the other side of the coin, it shows that when you are given data, you don't hear the entire message either. You trust the significant parts are caught in your 25-50 percent; however, imagine a scenario where they're most certainly not.

Listening is an ability that we would all be able to profit by improving. By improving as an audience, you can improve your efficiency, just like your capacity to impact, convince, and arrange. Additionally, you'll avoid conflict and misunderstandings. These are vital for work environment achievement!

Tip:

Great relational abilities require a significant level of self-awareness. Understanding your very own style of communicating will go far toward helping you to make great and lasting impressions with others.

About Active Listening

The best approach to improve your listening skills is to practice "active listening." This is the place you put forth a conscious effort to hear not just the words that someone else is stating- at the same time, more critically, the total message is being communicated.

To do this, you should focus on the other person very carefully.

You can't allow yourself to get diverted by whatever else might be happening around you, or by thinking of counter arguments while the other individual is as yet speaking. Nor would you be able to permit yourself to get bored, and lose center around what the other person is saying.

Tip:

In case you're finding it especially hard to focus on what somebody is stating, have a go at repeating their words intellectually as he says them – this will strengthen his message and help you to stay focused.

To improve your skills for truly listening, you have to tell the other individual that you are tuning in to what she is saying.

To understand the significance of this, inquire as to whether you've at any point been occupied with a discussion when you thought about whether the other individual was tuning in to what you were stating. You wonder if your message is getting over, or if it's even advantageous proceeding to talk. It wants to talk with a block wall, and it's something you need to keep away from.

Achieving Active Listening

Five vital active listening techniques can assist you with turning into a more effective listener:

1. Focus

Give the speaker your full focus and recognize the message. Perceive that non-verbal communication additionally "speaks" loudly.

- Look at the speaker directly.
- Put aside distracting thoughts.
- Don't intellectually set up a rebuttal!
- Avoid being diverted by natural variables. For instance, side discussions.
- "Listen" to the speaker's non-verbal communication.

2. Show That You're Listening

Utilize your non-verbal communication and signals to show that you are locked in.

- Nod occasionally

- Smile and utilize other facial expressions.

- Make sure that your stance is open and interesting.

- Encourage the speaker to proceed with little verbal remarks like truly, and "uh-huh."

3. Give Feedback

Our channels, suppositions, decisions, and beliefs can twist what we hear. As an audience, your job is to understand what is being said. They may expect you to think about what has been said, and pose more questions.

- Paraphrase what you've heard in your own (fair) words in order to reflect on it. "What I'm hearing is... "and "Sounds like you are stating... " are great ways to reflect.

- Ask inquiries to explain certain focuses. "What do you mean when you state...." "Is this what you mean?"

- Summarize the speaker's comments periodically.

Tip:

If you wind up reacting emotionally to what somebody stated, say as much. Furthermore, request more data: "I may not be understanding you effectively, and I wound up thinking about what you personally said. My take on what you said was 'XXX'- Is that what you intended?"

4. Don't Judge

Interrupting is an exercise in futility. It frustrates the speaker and limits a full understanding of the message.

- Allow the speaker to complete each point before asking questions.
- Don't hinder with counter arguments

5. React Appropriately

Active listening is intended to energize regard and understanding. You are picking up data and points of view. You don't include anything by attacking the speaker or, in any case, putting her down.

- Be real to life, transparent in your reaction.
- Assert your opinions, respectfully.
- Treat the other individual such that you figure she would need to be dealt with.

Key Points

It takes a great deal of concentration and determination to be an attentive person. Old habits are difficult to break, and on the off chance that your listening skills are as bad, the same number of individuals seem to be, at that point you'll have to do a lot of work to end these bad habits.

There are five key methods you can use to build up your active listening skills:

1. Pay attention
2. Show that you're tuning in.
3. Provide feedback.
4. Defer judgment.
5. Respond properly.

Begin utilizing undivided attention procedures today to improve as a communicator, improve your working environment efficiency, and grow better relationships.

Technique 8: How to use love bombing

If the developing number of matchmaking businesses and sites is any sign, nearly everybody who isn't seeing someone to be. Regardless of whether you need to be "in love" or "beloved," there's feasible a particular business out there someplace prepared to connect you with "similar adults," "discreet more seasoned noblemen," "country Romeos," "Christian singles," or whatever your "type" maybe. While communication technology and internet connections make it significantly simpler to discover potential partners, they also increment the risk that you will experience some not exactly perfect matches.

At the point when you openly advertise your interest in a sentimental relationship, you also signal your accessibility to any revolving around narcissists or social predators. If one detects that your guard is down, the individual in question may accept that you are a simpler objective for manipulation. And, one of the most effective methods for controlling a potential partner is through flattery and "love bombs."

Love bombarding feels better until it doesn't.

Love bombarding is the act of overpowering somebody with indications of adoration and attraction — think flattering remarks, tokens of love, or love notes on the mirror, kitchen table, or windshield, and you're starting to get the image. Its blossoms delivered at work with hearts dabbing the I's in your name. Its messages expand in frequency as they increase in romantic fervor. Its unexpected appearances intended to control you into spending more time with the aircraft — and, not incidentally, less time with others, or all alone.

We as a whole love to be adored, until it begins to want to be stalked.

At the point when somebody reveals to you exactly how special you are, it very well may be intoxicating, from the start. However, when an individual uses such remarks to maintain your emphasis prepared on that person or to hold you back if you've begun to chill out, it could be an instance of control. Not every person who says romantic things to you is a narcissist or predator, obviously, however, in case you feel that something simply isn't directly about the individual or your relationship, these constant reminders of "how great you are as one" — when you presume that you truly aren't — can be a push to keep you tethered. It's frequently the primary line utilized by a potential abuser.

For what reason do narcissists love bombs?

Narcissists specifically are known for their abilities at control, as much as their penchant for self-love.. They may utilize flattery and attention as tools to develop themselves as the ideal accomplice, the better to pick up your trust, warmth — and, at last, love. Narcissists regularly learn through experience that once partners see through their exteriors, the relationship may fall to pieces. When they have convinced you regarding how great you two are as one, a narcissist will attempt to shape your job in the relationship into an individual from their "supporting cast." For this and different reasons, narcissists normally battle to look after equivalent, mutually satisfying relationships.

Narcissists move rapidly to avoid identification, so the more somebody tries to flatter you into submission, the more diligently you have to investigate their motives.

If they say they adore me, how can they be narcissists?

Nonstop attention and day by day roses can sound appealing, yet if you were the object of this sort of warmth — from somebody you just met — you'd likely think it was more fearful than charming. The majority of us favor relationships that unfold in a generally steady manner. It's entirely expected to feel a surge of energy at each look, contact, or meeting toward the beginning of a new romantic relationship; however, when somebody's trying to move it along excessively quickly, it tends to be more than a little disconcerting.

At the point when we think about a love-bombing campaign, we have to remember that the ultimate objective is to win. At the point when the narcissist utilizes this system, the person does as such to catch their prey before the prey gets too wise to the game. It resembles when you're trying to entice your dog to come to you at the dog park — you utilize your best voice, pet names, and possibly draw out the extraordinary treats. You need to prevail upon your canine's trust and get him sufficiently close to you to snap the rope back on his collar. Narcissists will take the necessary steps to draw near enough to a romantic interest as fast as they can before their objective bolts.

People who are particularly high in the characteristic of narcissism, or the minority who are obsessive narcissists, may see others essentially as items to fulfill their longing for association or control.

Once more, there might be different clarifications for "love at first sight" stories: Sometimes, people genuinely do simply click from the beginning, and the relationship builds quickly, yet at the same time, at a solid pace that is agreeable for the two partners. Different occasions, a lovesick soul might be trying to do anything conceivable to pull in a partner. These cases regularly inspire feel sorry for in the sought after, though narcissistic pursuers create a different serious feeling — nervousness, once in a while dread, and now and again revulsion.

True love or manipulation: How can you tell?

There's saying that if something appears to be unrealistic, it presumably is. From days of yore, this saying has rung true: When somebody is incorporating you up with more than you realize that anybody could be — or gifting you in manners that are starting to feel too extravagant, or co-selecting your time since they need to spend such a large amount of theirs with you while secretly manipulating you to have brief period left over for friends or family — these are signs that the relationship isn't exactly as adjusted as it should be.

At the point when a relationship moves too quickly — or one partner tries to push it too forcefully — it's fundamental that you call your partner on it, and let the person in question know how you feel. If the person is happy to tune in and dial it back a notch, they might be motivated to give them, and the relationship, more opportunity to create. If a partner won't tune in to your protestations and just tries to excuse away the covering behavior, that is an indication that there's just liable to be not so much opportunity but rather more control later if you remain together.

At the point when you're anxious to discover a partner, it very well may be energizing to be the focal point of somebody you find appealing. Be careful, however, because narcissists can be talented at putting on the mask that their objective will find most attractive. Healthy whirlwind romances do occur, however in case you have a feeling that you're in a tornado of attention and it's more disrupting than not, it's an ideal opportunity to step back and have a discussion. If they're not able to change their behavior to match your requirements, it's unlikely that the person is a match for you.

Technique 9: Playing with Emotions

If you experience difficulty controlling your feelings, it is feasible for you to do as such. Figuring out how to get your feelings leveled out starts with the understanding that you are a finished and entire being. It is anything but difficult to think about your various self-regarding pieces of you. But, you are composed of something other than the individual pieces of yourself. Your body, your brain, thoughts, neurology, and emotions all work in tandem to make what your identity is and the truth that you experience. By understanding that you are more than the total of your parts, you can start the way toward figuring out how to control your feelings. Head NLP Life Coaching can give you a few strategies that you can use to help you through the procedure.

Why should you take control over your emotions?

One objective for figuring out how to get your feelings leveled out is to pick up the capacity to separate an event from your response to it. You would then be able to instruct yourself that you have different choices available to you.

Finding your emotional baseline

Each individual has a standard of feelings from which they work. Your emotional baseline is essentially the state of mind of your involvement with life, generally speaking. If you have a higher baseline, you will have a superior point of view toward your life and will experience fewer effects when negative things happen.

To make sense of what your pattern is, start by checking how you feel arbitrarily for the day. While you do this, focus on what's going on in your mind and body. Pay attention to the following things when you do:

- What is the time and the date?
- What are the physical emotions in your body?
- What is occurring in your brain?

After you have recorded these things around 20 or 30 different times, you should begin to see an example indicating your general state of mind. Understand that you are the main individual who can control your baseline. Get some information about what patterns you may have discovered. You should also analyze the thoughts and feelings that you experience often and consider whether they mirror the sorts of feelings and thoughts that you might want to have.

Boosting your baseline

If you find that, emotionally, your baseline is lower than you might want, you can find a way to raise it. One simple approach to do this is to adhere to the 5% rule, which is an NLP procedure that can support you. The thought behind the 5% rule is for you to give extra energy to each circumstance that you experience. For instance, if you are utilizing a treadmill, up to your speed by 5%. Try applying the 5% decide to everything that you do for 90 days to perceive how your mood improves.

Growing more emotional flexibility

Increasing your emotional flexibility can also assist you in mastering your feelings. Allowing yourself to experience a more extensive scope of feelings can be useful. You can do this by taking an improv class, watching goofy movies, acknowledging when others do something good, and allowing yourself to feel. Doing these sorts of things can allow you to experience more positive emotions.

Dealing with others

Others can't compel you to feel somehow. Even though you may have the option to make a logical connection between your feelings and what another person said to you, you are the person who has control over your feelings. At the point when you treat others as having the option to cause you to feel a specific way, your body will make you feel that specific feeling. Regardless of whether you feel as though somebody is making you feel bad, it is similarly as simple for you to cause yourself to feel great.

To change things, you should assume responsibility for your feelings. If you don't do as such, you won't have the option to control them. If somebody effectively tries to cause you to feel bad, you should do the opposite and relax and enjoy yourself. By and large, in case you remain quiet when another person is in an exceptionally charged state, the person will eventually also calm down.

Understand that a great many people are more stressed over themselves than about what you feel. If somebody says something that you dislike, recognize that what the individual said was likely unexpected. A great many people don't effectively try to cause others to suffer or to feel hopeless.

How to deal with challenges

Everybody needs to manage difficulties in their lives occasionally. Since you can expect that you will experience issues, it is a smart thought for you to find out how to manage them properly. At the point when you are faced with a challenge, bring it down to your sensory level. Describe it to yourself by just utilizing your faculties, for example, your sensation, sound-related, and visual faculties. This causes an issue to turn out to be more concrete so you can deal with it unbiasedly.

After you have found and defined the challenge, try to decide whether there is a conflict between it and your ideal emotional state. If there will be, there is something that you can do to fix it. You ought to also consistently work on trying to remove excess stress and tension from your body intentionally. Your body develops pressure trying to adjust to nature and your thoughts. At the point when you loosen up your body, it is simpler to keep control over the feelings that you feel.

Understand that the lion's share of things that happen don't quickly affect your well-being and health. Numerous individuals experience superfluous pressure since they feel that it is feasible for something bad to occur. You can rather decide to start arranging and progressing in the direction of having a superior circumstance than what you are in the present moment.

Dealing with habituated reactions

You may wind up responding to a circumstance before you can even set aside the effort to intentionally consider how you react. These types of reactions are shaped by habit. At the point when you are managing a habituated response, you can follow four stages to break the example, including the following:

- Identify the pattern
- Break it down to its littlest parts
- Identify the least factor parts
- Change the least factor parts

By and large, changing the least factor portions of an example will make the dynamic move.

Managing negative thoughts

Everybody has had thoughts that put them in bad moods. If you experience this, you may give it a push out of your brain, just for it to come back with more prominent power. This can exacerbate you, and make you feel worse than you at first did when the negative idea originally showed up. To deal with negative thoughts, you can start by not opposing them. Understand that your thoughts just exist within your psyche and are not real.

At the point when you have a negative idea, oblige it. Inserting a conscious purpose into an oblivious procedure can ruin it. Figure out how to play with negative thoughts when they come up. For instance, if you are flying on a plane, you may have a negative idea that you could pass on in a plane crash. However, the chances of this occurrence are very low. As per the National Safety Council, your odds of dying in a plane crash as a traveler is one out of 205,552.

If you end up stressing that you may pass on a plane, you can deliberately include the idea that you will push off and suffer eternal torture after you die. This causes the idea to appear to be more ridiculous. At the point when you start adding to a negative idea, it turns out to be more difficult for you to pay attention to it.

You can also consider the idea again, intentionally. At the point when you do that multiple times, you will become worn out on it, which will cause it to leave without anyone else. At the point when you find that you imagine all of the worst-case scenarios that could happen, you should start by growing the scope of potential outcomes. You can rather try to consider the entirety of the beneficial things that could occur rather than bad things. Everything relies upon how you decide to think and to utilize your mind.

Dealing with anger

It is hard for some individuals to get anger under control. For example, if another person cuts you off in traffic, you may feel angry. It is significant for you to understand that your anger is essentially an auxiliary feeling since it is a response to another occasion. At the point when you can recognize what is truly at the root of the anger that you are experiencing, you can acquire an understanding of what's going on and what necessities to change.

Dealing with your feelings can be a lifelong process. You need to work each day to keep control of your feelings. Recollect that your feelings are yours alone. When you start to point fingers at the individuals around you for your emotional state, you surrender your capacity to take care of business. In summary, do the following things to ace your feelings:

- Check your emotional express a few times consistently;
- Follow the 5% rule;
- Learn how to have more prominent adaptability in your feelings;
- When somebody tries to cause you to feel bad, focus on relaxing instead;
- Follow the four-advance procedure to deal with habituated responses;
- If you have a negative idea, play with it by adding to it or by effectively considering it through and through; and
- If you become irate, ask whether outrage is the most proper response.

If you can actualize these means, you will have the option to figure out how to control your feelings and to improve how you feel and a mind-blowing nature.

Technique 10: How to Magnify the Problems in the right way

The other week at work, we had a few issues with our email supplier. As the primary line of defense before getting our outsourced IT department involved, I get the brunt of everybody's frustrations. The issue itself was irregular, which for anybody that knows IT, realizes this is the worst type of problem to have. You need to make sense of the issue, yet try to make sense of what's going on precisely at the time that causes the issues. It could be as simple as a root activity running at that point. Obviously, it tends to be exceptionally hard to take care of the issue.

Magnifying your problems

Days like what was shown above are what make my job challenging. In my position, I never get congratulated when things are going right, since well, they should be running easily. In any case, if something goes wrong, alarms, bells, whistles, and people screaming my name happen continually.

While I understand my co-worker's failures with the issues, too often, they center eagerly around the issue, magnifying the issue.

What happens when you magnify your problems

At the point when you amplify your issues, they get greater than they truly are. On account of something worse, we exacerbate it multiple times by dwelling on it constantly. I used to do this constantly. I had a class in school that I hated. I needed to give presentations before the class, which I don't care about doing. As the weeks up to my presentation trickled away, everything I did was consider it. I thought to what extent I was going to talk for, how I would not like to do it, how I would have a dry mouth and sweat a lot, and what number of errors I would make.

At the point when it came time to make my presentation, I proceeded with it and lo and view, it wasn't that bad. I burned through such a large amount of my time and energy, magnifying this issue into something a lot greater than it truly was. Do you end up doing the same?

I have found that multiple times out of 100, the entirety of the bad" things I consider never happen as expected. It is simply me amplifying them to be greater than they are.

Change the script

Unfortunately, we as a whole will, in general, amplify the bad things in our lives. The presentation I needed to give. The IT issues piling up. The traffic jams. We never amplify the beneficial things in our lives. Think for brief how things would be if we magnified the great rather than the bad if we concentrated on the entirety of the beneficial things we have going for us. How might our children feel if we magnified how incredible they are by telling them and others concerning what they do? How might our mate feel if we did the same? How might we feel?

Final thoughts

In the end, we made sense of the issue with our email supplier following a couple of days. I needed to continually remind my collaborators that the issue wasn't as bad as they described it. Truly it was frustrating and a burden, yet they, much the same as me back in school, were magnifying our issues. When they understood this, they realized that the issue wasn't as bad as it appeared. Presently, I could get them to compliment the IT specialists when things are going right!

Technique 11: Illusion of choice

I wound up in a circumstance today that represented the influential idea of a particular mental model known as the dream of decision. This topic is familiar to any individual who has viewed The Matrix set of three, which was referenced in the scene where the architect describes that the way to keeping humankind subdued is giving a system that introduced the illusion of decision.

In reality, you think about the dream of a decision regardless of whether you don't have words for it. Imagine you are a young person and you need to study the violin. If you are allowed to decide to study the violin, you will appreciate it. Yet, if you are compelled to do it by your parents or your school area, you are probably going to revolt since you don't figure they ought to have the option to cause you to do something without wanting to. In this manner, you are bound to be emotionally fulfilled, happy, and, therefore, excel in the violin if you are allowed to decide to seek after it all alone.

I short-hand the deception of the decision as follows:

The illusion of decision is a mental model that states people are happy if they accept that they have power over their activities and can practice choice. If the free choice is denied, or denied, from an individual, the person in question will get angry or rebellious, regardless of whether the decision constrained upon him is identical from the one he would have chosen willingly.

As it were, if you purchase another vehicle since you need to purchase another vehicle, you're happy. If you purchase another vehicle since you got in a wreck, you most likely aren't satisfied. In the two cases, you are getting another vehicle, and the money related expense is probably going to the equivalent to you. The thing that matters is the illusion of having a choice.

The Illusion of Choice Shows Up at the Office This Morning

Today, Aaron plunks down to his work area and finds that his huge Power Mac with double 30″ top-notch Apple film screens has experienced a graphics card failure. Not cool. Along these lines, we talk about it. We conclude that as opposed to purchasing another graphics card for a few hundred dollars, I will simply upgrade my system by buying another one, at that point separated the parts in my old computer, which has similar specs to his, in a split second multiplying his memory, giving him four enormous internal hard-drives, with a working graphics card.

This will bring about his framework working just fine and having 2x the memory and 2x the extra room and me having a fresh out of the box new framework around my work area. Clearly, that leaves us with two extra 30″ HD films that won't be utilized, yet we'll make sense of that later. This ought to be acceptable, isn't that so? I ought to be happy, right? No. In any case, I'll find that in a moment.

I approved the organization to purchase another 27 inch iMac with 2.93 GHz Quad-Core i7 Intel processors, a 2 Terabyte hard drive, 8 Gigabytes of RAM, and a 1 GB ATI Radeon HD 5750 graphics card for my workstation. After Missouri deals charge, it came to $2,750.87. Since I did it through the American Express rewards program, I ought to get 4x focuses or 11,003 focuses. That is $110 more that I can trade out at a retailer if I ever recover them later on.

So not exclusively do all the wonderful things I simply described occur, I get significantly more rewards focused on spending later on. I ought to be glad, isn't that so? No.

You see, I had genuinely considered getting one of the new Apple systems half a month back just after my mother got hers. However, I chose, in what was a momentary quirk that I was going to deliberately deny myself and keep on building the organization's balance sheet. Presently, $2,750.87 is tiny contrasted with our incomes every year. I had disclosed to myself that it was an activity in self-control. It was "a thing" to me, similar to somebody who says, "No, I'm going to cause myself to go to the gym today," or "No, I am going to make myself cut the grass." Not too many weeks prior, when I sat down to the framework, I would be satisfied with myself since I believed that a modest piece of our asset report was developing since I was denying myself of something I needed.

When I settled on that decision, I had gotten underway with something known as "first conclusion bias." In any case, that is another psychological model for one more day.

The outcome is, even though everybody will be happier, we get sparkly new toys, and it will occur in time for Christmas, I'm discontent. The reason? It presently appears as though I need to do it as opposed to I need to do it. It is an illusion of choice, designed into human genetics that makes it tough, in any event, for me who knows about the wonder, to shake.

The Legend of Frugality ...

It helps me to remember a story Benjamin Graham wrote in his autobiography, which I read in my sophomore year of school. Even though he lived in a $12,000-a-month (in the 1930s!) townhouse in New York, he had a personal masseuse and lived incredibly well; he would here and there walk rather than taking the metro to save a nickel or two on tolls. He would feel guilty if he went through the cash.

Graham speculated that this personality trait– such guilt over small spending that doesn't appear to be significant – was a typical mental indication that stayed with the individuals who had manufactured their fortune. Somebody who acquired riches or who was going through another person's money wouldn't get it. A similar ability that made one wealthy – frugality – here and there runs practically like a working programming program. At times, it loads itself in any event, when you don't need it to or anticipate that it should do so ... sort of like when you intend to tap the Microsoft Excel symbol, /however, rather miss and hit the Firefox symbol.

The delight for an effective independent man or lady originated from the understanding that he could even now control his cash and that his cash wasn't controlling him. He wasn't, as it were, a slave to luxury. This is the illusion of choice.

Approaches to Combat the Illusion of Choice

There are a few different ways to battle the illusion of choice. The most well-known three are Hobson's choice, Morton's Fork, and Burdian's Ass. To outline:

Hobson's choice: A free decision where just a single option is offered; i.e., "accept the only choice available."

Morton's Fork: Is a decision between two similarly terrible other options (at the end of the day, a dilemma) or two lines of thinking that lead to the equivalent unpleasant end. It closely resembles the expression, "between the fallen angel and the dark blue ocean," and "in a tight spot."

Buridan's Ass is a delineation of a Catch 22 in theory in the origination of through and through freedom. It refers to a hypothetical dilemma wherein an ass is put exactly halfway between a pile of feed and a bucket of water. Since the Catch 22 accept the ass will consistently go to whichever is closer, it will die of both yearning and thirst since it can't settle on any reasonable choice to pick one over the other. The paradox is named after the fourteenth-century French savant Jean Buridan, whose way of thinking of good determinism, it satirizes.

Subsequently, to overcome the illusion of choice, you could introduce an enemy, or even your rebellious teenager, with a Hobson's decision framed option. "You can either tidy up your room and go out to see the films with your buddies, or you can leave your room as is and stay home. Your decision." Even so, the decisions have been limited; the battle will be far less because the individual accepted they had a small portion of choice to work out.

You could also present a bogus Morton's Fork situation. Let's assume you need something to go in a direction that is beneficial to you. By presenting two decisions, the two of which are unpleasant, that will result in the off chance that they don't follow your desires, you can cause them to accept they are choosing for themselves. For instance, if you somehow happened to infuse cash into an organization on the verge of bankruptcy. However, you need 80% of the ownership; you could essentially bring up fundamental facts :) If you don't do this, you'll lose everything. The bank will possess 100% of your organization, which will be closed down and stop to exist). If you do figure out how to hold tight, it will take a very long time to rebuild, and you'll have lost your family the entirety of their investment funds. The third other option, interestingly, doesn't look so awful (which gets into the contrast principle, another psychological model).

Finally, you could present a Buridan's Ass oddity if you don't need somebody to make a move. By overpowering them with decisions, all similarly engaging, however making them unrelated, you can adequately purpose them to make no move and along these lines lose all favorable positions.

I once knew an effective entrepreneur that was so conflicted about what to do in regards to the fate of his business that he sat by and over a 5 to multi-year time frame, observed almost every penny he had amassed go down the channel. He couldn't settle on a decision. Thus his lack of decision became, basically, a kind of decision. He just settled on a choice once the banks were breathing down his neck; however, by then, it was past the point of no return. His savings were gone, his pay drained, and a fortune wasted. It was deplorable.

I think he wound up recovering, or at any rate, lived fairly. However, it was still unnecessary.

The "Thinking Outside about the Box" Cliché

The rare, effective character will immediately perceive that the decisions are not, actually, limited.

The cliché for this is "thinking outside about the crate." I think anyone would agree that a lot of my prosperity has originated from having the option to make associations others don't and seeing decisions they don't realize exist. The vast majority trust you need to "find a decent line of work with benefits" to survive. Or then again, "If you get a degree in enterprise, you will be an achievement." Instead, I tuned in to the smarter men, Peter Lynches and Charlie Mungers, who discussed the significance of rationale, morals, and old-style human sciences instruction.

Technique 12: The simplicity is the key

Genuine and lasting happiness isn't the consequence of collecting more. Happy people know that happiness originates based on what's created inside and not from their outside condition.

Our reality resembles an enormous commercial center, and the temptation is all over the place. Stuff costs cash, however. It can also require us emotional currency, since we may begin to perceive what we possess as being more significant than the people in our lives. This is the moment that individuals become powerless and can become unhappy.

It's a great opportunity to hinder those consistent wants to purchase things and begin putting resources into yourself and your connections. We chase the material by putting extended periods in work, shuffling entangled calendars, and protracted plans for the day. We become involved with bringing home the bacon, rather than making a life.

We try to fulfill ourselves with sensory pleasures trusting that they will carry us more like a condition of peace. However, genuine and lasting happiness originates from expelling things we don't require, not storing them. Joy comes to us when we detox ourselves from fear, uncertainty, negativity, and desires. Past that lies a perspective characterized by virtue, where delight exists in its most perfect structure.

Give it a shot for yourself. Wake up, thankful for all that you have, and fight the temptation to purchase useless things that you realize you needn't bother with.

In the cutting edge world, we are constantly informed that we need either. Plugs on TV are continually selling things from nightfall 'till first light. On gigantic billboards as we drive to work there are advertisements, and up spring advertisements on each site and online life stage that we visit. We are continually bombarded, yet it's essential to oppose these temptations and take a step back.

Before you buy something, you ought to ask yourself these questions...

- Will this thing truly fulfill me?
- Do I really need it?
- Does it fill a need or present to me a sense of joy?

Avoid stores except if you're going out in light of a particular buy, as you could turn out with a lot of things that you didn't need!

Adopting simplicity starts with a quick environment. Check out you and check whether there's anything you can do to decrease the mess in your home, for example, stacks of magazines, books, desk work, and garments. Tidy up and arrange your environment with the goal that you have fewer distractions.

Clear a space in your mind

Getting out of your inward space is more significant than tidying your outside space. Step out of your mind and analyze your thoughts dispassionately. Work towards disposing of any troubling or negative thoughts that are causing you stress and undue anxiety.

Concentrate more on yourself as well as other people, and not the things they have. Free you from your assets, and you'll experience life through an alternate focal point. Free yourself from the weight of assets that aren't essential to who we truly are. You'll feel vastly improved over the long run and will have the option to focus on what your identity is, the thing that you need, and, in particular, you'll be happy.

Technique 13: The Power of Touch

You're in a packed metro vehicle on a Tuesday morning, or maybe on city transport. Still-sluggish suburbanites calmed by vibrations, stay quieted, yet quietly broadcast their thoughts.

A baby in his carriage takes a look at his fellow passengers, brows stitched with concern. He goes to Mom for reassurance, connecting a little hand. She quietly takes it, presses, and discharges. He relaxes, smiles, turns away—at that point back to Mom. She takes his hand once more: squeeze and release.

A twenty-something in a skirt and coat sits stiffly, a calfskin bound portfolio on her lap. She over and over pushes a couple of blonde wisps off her face, at that point contacts her neck, her intuitive developments both uncovering and relieving her anxiety about her 9 a.m. meet.

A couple propped against a pole shares thoughts and feelings of friendship; she rubs his arms with her hands, he nestles his face in her hair.

A middle-aged woman, squished into a corner, without a doubt knocks the youngster next to her with some accidental elbows and hips. The message is made clear; he immediately adjusts to make room.

Testing our capacity to convey non-verbally is not another mental tack; analysts have since quite a while ago reported the mind's complex feelings and wants that our posture, movements, and expressions uncover. However, up to this point, the possibility that individuals can give and interpret emotional content through another nonverbal methodology—contact—appeared to be risky, even to analysts, for example, DePauw University clinician Matthew Hertenstein, who studies it. In 2009, he showed that we have an inborn capacity to unravel feelings through touch alone. In a progression of studies, Hertenstein had volunteers attempt to impart a list of feelings to a blindfolded outsider exclusively through touch. Numerous members were fearful of the examination. "This is a touch-phobic culture," he says. "We're not used to touching strangers, or even our friends, essentially."

But, contact they did—it was, all things considered, for science. The outcomes recommend that for all our alertness about contacting, we come outfitted with a capacity to share and get emotional signs exclusively thusly. Members shared eight clear feelings—fear, anger, appall, love, appreciation, compassion, happiness, and misery—with exactness rates as high as 78 percent. "I was amazed," Hertenstein admits. "I figured the precision would be at chance level," around 25 percent.

Past examinations by Hertenstein and others have created similar findings abroad, remembering for Spain (where individuals were greater at delivering through touch than in America) and the U.K. Research has additionally been directed in Pakistan and Turkey. "Wherever we've examined this, people appear to be ready to do it," he says.

Surely, we seem, by all accounts, to be wired to interpret a few of our fellow people. An investigation giving proof of this capacity was distributed in 2012 by a group that utilized fMRI outputs to measure brain activation in individuals being contacted. The subjects, every hetero male, were demonstrated a video of a man or a lady who was purportedly contacting them on the leg. Subjects evaluated the experience of male touch as less lovely. Mind checks uncovered that a piece of the brain called the essential somatosensory cortex reacted more forcefully to a lady's touch than to a man's. In any case, here's the turn: The videos were fake. It was always a lady touching the subjects.

The outcomes were alarming because the essential somatosensory cortex had been thought to encode just fundamental characteristics of touch, for example, smoothness or weight. That its movement changed relying upon whom subjects accepted was contacting them proposes that the emotional and social parts of touch are everything except inseparable from physical sensations. "At the point when you're being moved by someone else, your mind isn't set up to give you the target characteristics of that touch," says study co-author Michael Spezio, a therapist at Scripps College. "The whole experience is influenced by your social assessment of the individual touching you."

If touch is a language, it appears we instinctively realize how to utilize it. In any case, it's an ability we granted. At the point when they had gotten some more information about it, the subjects in Hertenstein's investigations reliably underestimate their capacity to convey using touch—even while their activities proposed that touch perhaps in real be more flexible than voice, facial expression, and different modalities for expressing emotion.

"With the face and voice, as a rule, we can recognize only a couple of positive signals that are not confused for one another," says Hertenstein. For instance, happiness is the main positive feeling that has been dependably decoded in studies of the face. Then, his exploration shows that touch can communicate different positive feelings: satisfaction, love, appreciation, and compassion. Researchers used to think contact was a method for upgrading messages motioned through discourse or non-verbal communication, "however it appears rather that touch is a substantially more nuanced, sophisticated, and exact approach to convey feelings," Hertenstein says.

It might also speed up communication: "In case you're sufficiently close to contact, it's frequently the easiest way to signal something," says Laura Guerrero, coauthor of Close Encounters: Communication in Relationships, who investigates non-verbal and emotional communication at Arizona State University. This immediacy is especially vital with regards to holding. "We feel progressively associated with somebody if they contact us," Guerrero notes.

There's no expression book to decipher the language of touch; if anything, specialists have barely started recording its punctuation and vocabulary. "We found that there is a wide range of approaches to demonstrate a given feeling through touch," Hertenstein notes. Additionally, how a touch gets interpreted is very setting dependent. "Regardless of whether we're at the specialist's office or in a club assumes a huge job in how the brain reacts to a similar kind of contact," Spezio clarifies. Analyzing a portion of the remarkable ways that we share and bond through touch (and how we build up the ability to do as such) uncovers the adaptability of this instrument and recommends approaches to utilize it. There's a lot to be picked up from embracing our tactile sense—specifically, progressively positive cooperation and a more profound feeling of association with others.

Learning the Language of Touch

We start accepting material signals even before birth, as the vibration of our mom's heartbeat is intensified by amniotic liquid. No big surprise then that touch assumes an essential job in parent-kid connections from the beginning: "It's a fundamental channel of communication with parents for a kid," says San Diego State University School of Communication emeritus teacher Peter Andersen, author of Nonverbal Communication: Forms and Functions.

A mother's touch upgrades connection among mother and youngster; it can signify security ("You're protected; I'm here") and, contingent upon the sort of touch, it can produce positive or negative feelings. (Playing pat-a-cake satisfies newborn children, while an unexpected crush from Mom frequently signals a warning not to communicate with another object). The mother's touch even appears to moderate pain when newborn children are given a blood test. College of Miami School of Medicine's Tiffany Field, chief of the Touch Research Institute, has connected touch, as a back rub, to a large number of advantages, including better rest, decreased irritability, and expanded friendliness among newborn children—just as improved development of preemies.

We're never contacted as much as when we're youngsters, which is the point at which our solace level with physical contact, and with physical closeness as a rule (what researchers call proxemics), creates. "The way that there's a ton of social variety in comfort with contact proposes it's predominantly learned," Andersen says.

Warm atmospheres will in general produce societies that are more liberal about contact than colder regions (might suspect Greeks versus Germans, or Southern neighborliness versus New England stoicism). There are various hypotheses regarding why, including the way that a higher surrounding temperature expands the availability of skin ("It pays to contact someone if there's skin showing or they're wearing light apparel through which they can feel the touch," Andersen says); the impact of daylight on mood ("It increases friendliness and lustfulness—lack of daylight can make us discouraged, with less associations"); and transient examples ("Our precursors would in general relocate to a similar atmosphere zone they originated from. The upper Midwest is intensely German and Scandinavian, while Spaniards and Italians went to Mexico and Brazil. That impacts the brand of touch").

What goes on in your home also assumes a job. Andersen takes note of that nonbelievers, and skeptics contact more than religious types, "likely because religions frequently train that a few sorts of touch are inappropriate or sinful." Tolerance for contact isn't stone, in any case. Spend time in another culture, or even with tricky feely friends, and your attitude toward contact can change.

When we're adults, a large portion of us has discovered that contacting will, in general, up the ante, especially with regards to a feeling of availability. In any event, brief contact with an outsider can have a quantifiable impact, both encouraging and upgrading participation. In a study done in 1976, clerks at a college library returned library cards to students either with or without quickly contacting the student's hand. Student interviews uncovered that those who'd been contacted assessed the agent and the library all the better—the impact held in any event when students hadn't seen the touch.

Later examinations have discovered that apparently irrelevant contacts yield greater tips for servers that people shop and purchase more if a store greeter moves them and that strangers are bound to support somebody if a touch goes with the request. Consider it the human touch, a short update that we are, at our center, social animals. "Bunches of times in these studies people don't remember being contacted. They simply feel there's an association; they feel that they like that person more," Guerrero says.

Exactly how solid is contact's holding advantage? To discover, a group driven by the University of Illinois at Urbana-Champaign clinician Michael Kraus followed physical contact between colleagues during NBA games (consider each one of those chest knocks, high fives, and backslaps). The study revealed that the more on-court contact there was right off the bat in the season, the more successful groups and people were via season's end. The impact of touch was free of player performance, dispensing with the likelihood that players contact more if they're more highly skilled or compensated better.

"We were surprised. Contact anticipated performance over all the NBA groups," says Kraus. "Ballplayers in some cases don't have the opportunity to express an urging word to a colleague; rather, they built up this incredible repertoire of touch to convey rapidly and precisely," he clarifies, including that touch can almost certainly improve performance over any helpful setting. Similarly, as with our primate family members, who strengthen social bonds by preparing one another, in people, "contact reinforces connections and is a marker of closeness," he says. "It expands participation, but, on the other hand, is a marker of how strong bonds are between individuals."

If a post-bounce back slap on the back of the brush of a hand while delivering a bill can help all of us show signs of improvement, it might be because "when you stimulate the pressure receptors in the skin, you lower pressure hormones," says the Touch Research Institute's Field. Simultaneously, warm touch stimulates the arrival of the "cuddle hormone," oxytocin, which upgrades a feeling of trust and attachment.

The release also clarifies our penchant for self-stroking, which we do many occasions every day as a calming mechanism. "We do a great deal of self-contacting: flipping our hair, embracing ourselves," Field notes. Other regular practices incorporate kneading our temples, rubbing our hands, or stroking our necks. Evidence supports that it's viable: Self-kneading has appeared to slow the pulse and lower the degree of the stress hormone cortisol.

A Touch of Love

Each night at sleep time, DePauw's Hertenstein gives his young child a back rub. "It's a holding open door for both of us. Oxytocin levels go up, pulses go down, all these brilliant things that you can't see." Moments like these also uncover the equal idea of touch; he says: "You can't contact without being touched. A great deal of those equivalent helpful physiological outcomes transpires, the individual doing the touching."

Indeed, when we're the ones starting contact, we may receive no different rewards as those we're contacting. For instance, Field's examination has uncovered that an individual giving massage experiences as extraordinary a decrease in stress hormones as the individual on the less than desirable end. "Studies have indicated that an individual giving an embrace gets the same amount of advantage as an individual being hugged," she includes.

Also, contacting someone else isn't only a single direction road with regards to signaling; besides sending them a message, it uncovers an extraordinary arrangement of data about their perspective, Hertenstein notes. It is safe to say that they are available to contact, or do they pull away? Is it true that they are loose or tense? Is it true that they are warm—or maybe cold and moist? "In some cases, I'll contact my better half and can tell in a split second—regardless of whether my eyes are shut—that she's focused on," he says. "You can detect that through muscle tightness and contraction, and this sort of data can manage our behavior with that individual—it impacts what we think, how we see what they state."

Maybe because touch influences both the individual being touched and the one is doing the touching, it is one of the most basic methods for cultivating and communicating intimacy in a romantic relationship. One paper proposed a grouping of 12 practices of expanding closeness that couples, for the most part, follow:

After the initial three (eye-to-body contact, eye-to-eye to eye connection, and talking), the remaining nine include contacting (beginning with holding hands, at that point kissing, and in the long run sexual closeness). "Contact works a bit differently depending upon the phase of the relationship," says Guerrero. "In the first place, it's sort of exploratory. Will the other person respond if I contact?" As the relationship advances, contacting starts to spike. "You see bunches of open touch," she notes, "Individuals holding hands the entire time they're as one or with their arms around one another's shoulders. It signals they're intensifying the relationship."

In any case, it would be a mix-up to believe that the measure of contacting couples does keep on following an escalating trajectory. Research including the perception of couples in broad daylight and investigation of their self-reports shows that the measure of touching rises at the beginning of a relationship tops someplace from the get-go in a marriage, and then decreases. After some time, romantic partners change the measure of touching they do, up-or downshifting their touch to draw nearer to their loved one's habits. Failure to join in a typical safe place will, in general, wreck a relationship right off the bat, while among couples in long haul relationships, touching arrives at an almost one-to-one ratio.

While couples who are happy with one another will in general touch more, the genuine pointer of a healthy long-term bond isn't how frequently your partner contacts you yet how regularly the person touches you because of your touch. "The more grounded the communication, the more probable somebody is to report emotional intimacy and fulfillment with the relationship," Guerrero says. Also, with numerous things seeing someone, fulfillment is as much about what we partner for our partner as about what we're getting.

The Laws of Social Contact

The most significant things we uncover through touch: "presumably our level of predominance and our level of intimacy," Andersen says. Take, for instance, the handshake, one of only a handful barely any circumstances in which it's OK to reach an outsider. It's a significant chance of communicating something specific about yourself. "A limp handshake signifies vulnerability, low eagerness, introversion," Andersen says, while a viselike hold can be interpreted as a sign that you're trying to rule. "You need to have a firm yet not a bone-crushing handshake," he prompts since it's smarter to be seen as excessively warm as a distant person. "We like individuals to have a sort of medium-elevated level of warmth," Andersen says. "An individual who touches a lot says, 'I'm a friendly, close individual.' More touch-situated specialists, educators, and managers get higher evaluations."

In any case, outside of intimate connections, the outcomes of sending an inappropriate message additionally increase. "Touchy people are facing some challenge that they may be seen as being over-the-top or harassing," says Andersen. "Physical contact can be creepy; it tends to be threatening." Context matters, which is the reason we have leads about who we can contact, where, and when. "For the most part, starting from the shoulder to the hand are the main acceptable areas for touch," in any event between casual associates, as indicated by Andersen. "The back is low in nerve endings, with the goal that's OK as well."

There are other contextual considerations too. Various societies and people have diverse resilience levels for touch. Same-sex and other gender contacts have various implications. At that point, there's the nature of the touch, the span, the force, the conditions. "It's a complex matrix," Andersen says. A fast touch and discharge—like a tap on a cubicle mate's shoulder to stand out enough to be noticed—no issue. But, a slap on the shoulder could be effectively misjudged. ("Most instances of lewd behavior include stroking contacts," notes Andersen.)

A touch will normally appear to be more intimate if it is joined by different signs, for example, a drawn out look, or if it is held a moment excessively long. In the meantime, a crush on the arm could be an indication of sympathy or support, however in the event that it doesn't end rapidly and is joined by extraordinary eye to eye connection, it can seem to be a squeeze of aggression. Condition changes things as well: On the playing field, a man may feel great giving his colleague a pat on the butt for occupation very much done, however, that congratulatory signal wouldn't do excessively well in the workplace.

Extremely, the main principle that ensures communicating by contact won't push you into difficulty is this: Don't do it, which likely holds true in the worker handbook for your work environment. In any case, leaving your mankind each time you venture out from home isn't extremely engaging. Andersen's somewhat less stringent rules for contact: Outside of your closest relationships, stick to the protected areas of shoulders and arms (handshakes, high fives, backslaps). In the workplace, it's in every case better for a subordinate, instead of a prevalent or manager, to initiate.

In case there's a most proper time to communicate through touch, it's likely when somebody needs consoling. "Research shows that touch is the ideal approach to comfort," says Guerrero. "If you ask individuals how they'd comfort somebody in a given circumstance, they will come in general list taps, embraces, and various types of touch practices more than anything else. Indeed, even other gender friends, for instance, who for the most part don't contact a great deal so they won't send the wrong signals, won't stress over being misinterpreted," she says.

Perhaps that is because there are times—during exceptional grief or fear, yet additionally in delighted snapshots of happiness or love—when just the language of touch can completely express what we feel.

Technique 14: How to be Silent at times

Utilizing silence to get results

People abhor silence how nature severely abhors a vacuum and race to fill it with a similar energetic willingness. Quiet feeds our minds and incites a wide range of anxious conjurations. In case we're sharp about it, in any case, we can use these negative responses to make positive worth.

Quietness can motivate students to endeavor to answer questions. As I gained from my experience as an occupant, if you can become open to persevering through the harsh thud of silence once you've thrown out a question, training yourself to hold up a long ways past the point that feels good, somebody will break before you do and try to answer your question. And, in any event, one investigation has demonstrated we're bound to remember the right response to a question in case we're told it in the wake of guessing incorrectly than if we're told it in the wake of declining to dare to say it by any means.

Quietness can make you more productive at your job. That is if you can compel yourself to tune in before surrendering to the drive to talk. My better half, a business land dealer, utilizes quiet when she leads a "discovery session" with her customers, saying nothing regarding herself or her systems for finding them office space until after she's listened altogether to their business necessities and issues they find significant. By what other method, she argues, would she be able to be certain when she does propose space arrangements that she's gathering her customers' needs? One would think each land agent would do this, yet she winds up continually astounded (and satisfied) by what a small number of her rivals do. Skirting this progression isn't restricted to the business world, either. At the point when patients decline prescribed tests or treatments, specialists commonly react by launching into arguments intended to make their advice clearer. Rarely do I see a specialist delay first to question as to why the patient is won't. But, when I quiet myself and listen first, I frequently become familiar with my assumptions regarding why I'm being refused are wrong. One patient with a clear requirement for a cardiovascular catheterization rejected it not out of a fear of possible complications as I'd assumed, but since he didn't figure, he could lie level for the necessary six hours a while later. Listening initially empowers me to either ease a patient's unjustified fears or understand their authentic complaints. Furthermore, if a protest is authentic, how might I conclude how to manage it—try to counter it or make an elective suggestion—if I don't have a clue what it is?

Silence is power

With the caveat that power can always be abused, the compelling utilization of quietness can present numerous blessings, boss among them:

The capacity to listen effectively. Few do it well. The greater part of us participates in listening just as a method for holding up until it's our chance to talk. If you can't avoid contemplating what you need to state when tuning in, center rather explicitly on being quiet. You'll be astounded how much your capacity to think will improve. And if you can quit concentrating on what you need to state when tuning in (don't stress; it won't go anyplace you can't find it) and rather focus completely on what's being said to you, at that point quietness won't simply present to you a new skill; it will bring you knew information. Remember that listening is more remarkable than talking. You don't master anything by saying something (which by definition you know). Furthermore, how regularly would we say we are extremely ready to impact another's behavior or beliefs by what we state?

Away from into the hearts of others. Quietness gets you off the beaten path and makes a space others will fill in with themselves. An individual's character becomes apparent in minor hours to days. Evaluating an individual's character, then again, takes a long time to years. In any case, individuals remain at each minute. An offhand comment made when you initially meet somebody might be, everything considered, clearly illustrative of an enormous character defect (or ideals). If you utilize quietness to listen carefully to what individuals state as well as how they state it, you'll see they'll part with themselves to you continually and empower you to understand their character far sooner than you would have the option to something else. Having had long periods of work on collaborating with and watching details in our kindred people's expression and tone has made our instinct undeniably more exact than we regularly accept. It just requires you're quiet to give full play to its capacity.

Attractiveness. People need more than anything to be heard and understood and will discover any individual who gives them that feeling powerfully charismatic.

Self-control. Think the amount more in charge you'd show up as well as really be if your first reaction after hearing or seeing something that starts a strong response in you wasn't to lash out genuinely yet rather become—silent. Silence is an astounding substitute for self-control, making its appearance, yet after some time and with training its substance too.

Intelligence. When facing another challenge, making quiet your first reaction allows you to reflect before you talk, improving the probability that what you state and do will be on track, intelligent, and helpful. Further, quiet reflection advances the appropriate use of what we bring in medication as a "tincture of time." If you fight the urge to leap energetically at the primary minute an issue emerges, the issue regularly fixes itself. In medication, as throughout everyday life, now and again, the wisest action is none at all.

Before that discussion during my residency, I'd just thought about quiet as something to be delighted in isolation and avoid from within sight of others. Presently I consider it a tool I can use to make myself more effective at my particular employment and all the more understanding of others and along these lines more emotional, wiser, and happier. Simply think about how the world would be extraordinary if we as a whole spent more time listening. At any rate, it would be a whole lot quieter.

Technique 15: Do it gradually

Remaining focused can be difficult, yet it tends to be especially testing when you are surrounded by constant distraction. In the present constantly associated world, diversions are just a click away. In any event, during calm minutes, distraction is readily available as you end up checking your Facebook or trying to get that elusive Pokémon.

The capacity to focus on something in your condition and direct mental effort toward it is basic for learning new things, achieving objectives, and performing admirably over a wide variety of circumstances. Regardless of whether you are trying to complete a report at work or contending in a marathon, your capacity to the center can mean the difference between success and failure.

Techniques:

1. Start by Assessing Your Mental Focus

Before you begin moving in the direction of improving your mental focus, you should start by surveying exactly how heavy your mental focus is at the present minute.

If the main arrangement of statements appears to be more your style, at that point, you most likely as of now, have genuinely good concentration abilities, yet you could be much more grounded with a little practice.

If you recognize more with the second arrangement of statements, at that point, you most likely need to take a shot at your mental focus a lot. It may require some time, however practicing some great habits and being aware of your distractibility can help.

2. Eliminate Distractions

Let it out; you saw this one coming. While it might sound obvious, individuals frequently think little of exactly what number of distractions keep them from focusing on the job that needs to be done. Such intrusions may come as a radio blaring out of sight or maybe an upsetting collaborator who continually drops by your desk area to visit.

Minimizing these sources of distraction frequently sounds simpler than it truly is. While it may be as basic as turning off the television or radio, you may think that it's substantially more challenging to deal with an interrupting on associate, mate, kid, or roommate.

3. Focus on One Thing at a Time

While performing multiple tasks may appear to be an incredible method to complete a lot done quickly, things being what they are, individuals are entirely bad at it. Juggling multiple tasks without a moment's delay can drastically eliminate profitability and makes it a lot harder to focus on the genuinely significant subtleties.

Think about your attention as a spotlight. If you sparkle that focus on one specific area, you can see things. If you somehow managed to try to spread that equivalent measure of light over a huge dull room, you may rather just impression the shadowy outlines.

Some portion of improving your mental focus is tied in with benefiting as much as possible from the assets you have accessible. Stop multitasking and rather focus on each thing in turn.

4. Live at the Time

It's difficult to remain mentally focused when you are ruminating about the past, worrying over the future, or blocked out of the present minute for some other explanation. You have likely heard people talk about the significance of "being available." It's everything about taking care of interruptions, regardless of whether they are physical (your cell phone) or mental (your nerves) and being completely mentally occupied with the current moment.

This thought of being available is also essential for recovering your mental focus. Remaining occupied with the present time and place keeps your attention sharp, and your mental resources focused on the details that truly matter at a particular point in time.

5. Practice Mindfulness

Mindfulness is an interesting topic right now, and all things considered. Regardless of the way that people have practiced forms of mindfulness meditation for a great many years, its numerous medical advantages are as of late beginning to be understood.

In one investigation, scientists had HR experts take part in recreations of the kind of complex performing various tasks they occupied with every day at work. These assignments must be finished in a short time and include noting telephones, scheduling meetings, and writing reminders with sources of data pouring in from various sources, including calls, messages, and instant messages.

6. Have a go at taking a Short Break

Have you, at any point, tried to focus on something very similar for a significant period? Sooner or later, your center begins to separate, and it turns out to be increasingly harder to dedicate your mental resources to the task. That, however, your performance suffers thus.

Traditional explanations in psychology have recommended this is because of attentional resources being depleted. Yet, a few specialists accept that it has more to do with the brain's tendency to disregard sources of constant stimulation.

So whenever you are working on a lengthy task, for example, setting up your assessments or reading for a test, make sure to offer yourself an occasional mental break. Move your regard for something inconsequential to the job that needs to be done, regardless of whether it is just for a couple of seconds. These short moments of break may imply that you can maintain your mental focus sharp and your performance high when you genuinely need it.

Technique 16: Repeat a few words

There was some daylight this end of the week while I was composing this! In any event here on the radiant south coast of England, there was. I went out walking along the oceanfront with my partner Sara on Saturday morning, and it was great; the feeling of sunshine all over, the smell of the air, the destinations of others out on the town and happy, the neighborhood land train was shuttling people, and their energized youngsters to and fro from Bournemouth wharf to Boscombe Pier and my faculties were filled – a significant occasion for human neurophysiology (mine anyway!)

The entertaining thing is, later on, that night, when my friends were kidding about my pink-hued brow, I disclosed to them that I was truly anticipating summer. As I spoke, I felt the sun on me, imagined the enjoyment I would have on the seashore, remembered the smell, the stunning feeling of satisfaction that I get from being there, just by anticipating it all.

A natural marvel we can duplicate with NLP systems. NLP represents neuro-etymological programming, which is only a system for helping make changes. We abbreviate it to NLP for easy understanding.

Without acknowledging it, the time I had spent on the seafront prior that day had gone about as a stay for the great experience, which quickly followed it. Whenever I saw and heard the experience, yet in my mind, my nervous system science went "I realize what happens now" and began to deliver the exceptional physical reactions that it 'knew' were coming next.

In the field of NLP, a stay is any representation in the human sensory system that triggers some other representation. For example, the word 'sex' will promptly trigger pictures, sounds, and so on related to that word. The word 'chocolate' will trigger various associations. I am not very sure which of those will make the most intense feelings, however!

These words are stays. Grapples don't need to be words; they can be a wide range of things.

With NLP, we identify that anchors can work in any authentic framework (i.e., sight, sound, feeling, smell, taste.) Let me give you a few models;

Tonal: By that, I mean, for instance, the exceptional way someone, in particular, has of saying your name, similar to when a friend or relative says it. My mom yelling my name from the depths of my home when I was a kid regularly signaled the way that she had found something that I experienced that meant difficulty for me! "Adam!" regularly caused me to feel what I was coming up for.

Material: The impact of a particular kind of handshake for instance, or the impression of a reassuring hug compared with a loving cuddle. Revives a wide range of great feelings.

Visual: The manner in which individuals react to specific things of apparel. I as of late ate with a group of my friends from the town where I grew up and a few of them commented on the coat I was wearing. Presently, at whatever point they see it, it helps them to remember those remarks and discusses their smile.

Olfactory: Like when you smell a specific sort of nourishment being cooked, can suddenly have you remember when you were in the school cafeteria.

Gustatory: The flavor of your favorite food or how certain foods can cause you to recall how you felt when you had it previously. Perhaps like when you were given soup and a big helping of love and sympathy when you were youthful and off school since you were ineffective. I know each time I eat Heinz Tomato soup, it helps me to remember only that.

By and by, in the field of NLP, an anchor is any representation in the human sensory system that triggers some other representation. It is conceptually like Pavlovian conditioning (ie. Bells and salivating hounds; some of Pavlov's findings feature in the field of NLP.

While the anchor I made for the oceanfront was unexpected, it is workable for you to utilize this NLP technique to stay yourself intentionally. Have a go at this and gain proficiency with this NLP procedure for yourself... ...

Firstly, think about an event when you had an exceptionally pleasurable, positive, or agreeable experience. See what you saw at that point (watching out through your own eyes), hear what you heard and feel what you felt. As you feel the sensations increase in power, press the thumb and index finger of your left hand gently together for a couple of seconds; at that point, release them. Presently 'break your state' (E.g., by remembering what you had for lunch yesterday.) Squeeze your thumb and index finger together again, gently beating them. The state will return.

To benefit as much as possible from securing a NLP, it is essential to truly take part in the experience and make it wonderfully vivid in your brain and to then also put effort into reviewing it when you initially enact your NLP stay for a couple of times. Imagine how incredible this can be the point at which you need to feel great if you are home, feeling gloomy. Rather than going after the chocolate, you can begin to activate your "vibe great" stay.

Each time you need to get motivated to work out, simply initiate your eagerness to stay. It is a fundamental strategy of NLP.

This is a simple, however amazing NLP system that can empower you to approach the states and assets you need when you need them. The utilization of the thumb and forefinger is a case of a tactile anchor. However, you can utilize any representation to stay something for yourself or another person.

Rules for setting stays with NLP;

To get a 'strong' anchor for an encounter, it is crucial to:

- Ensure that you have an amazing case of the experience to work with.

- Anchor in whatever number authentic frameworks as could be allowed (visual, sound-related, kinaesthetic, and so forth).
- Set the stay not long before the experience tops.
- When you activate the anchor, do it precisely. Be exact!
- With material (kinaesthetic) anchors, beating the stay can assist with keeping up the experience

One of the individuals who went ahead one of my NLP instructional classes was especially taken with securing. Soon after the NLP training, one morning, his significant other offered to make him some tea, and as she did as such, he tenderly tapped the side of his cup with his ring. He repeated this the following scarcely any occasion she made him some tea. After a while, all he needed to do was tap the side of his cup subtly with his ring, and she would suddenly offer to get him some tea!! Naughty utilization of NLP, Eh?! Just by making a sensory representation (tapping the cup) that agreed with her creation tea, he was soon ready to utilize that portrayal as a trigger for what he needed. He did, in the long run, share his NLP anchoring experience with his wife, and you can be certain he makes significantly more tea than she does now!

Presently I realize that at this point, some of you might be thinking, "However, isn't that manipulative?!?" One answer is, "Indeed, so use it for doing great stuff!"

Another answer is "no." It is not any more manipulative than making yourself look great and smell good when you go out. In those circumstances, you are trying to get individuals to think the best of you and have a good reaction to you, a reaction that you are trying to anchor through your decision of clothing, grooming and smelly perfume.

Here are a portion of the sorts of things that I make a special effort to utilize NLP to anchor at whatever point I see them or experience them:

- Smiles.
- Laughter.
- Excitement

- Confidence
- Good emotions
- Good performance
- Anything that looks great, helpful, or fun; Achievement and success are particularly valuable for preventing smoking, decreasing weight, or developing in certainty.

It's going on constantly in any case:

As I said toward the start, mooring with NLP is a normally occurring phenomenon at any rate. You are presented to it constantly in all that you do. Everybody is doing this stuff constantly, regularly without truly knowing it. All I am welcoming you to do is to get conscious of the anchors that you and others are setting (perhaps utilizing NLP) and to begin utilizing them deliberately to get great outcomes, as opposed to get whatever you get randomly. Use NLP with care.

Making this a step further;

As of late, I was working with a group of related staff individuals concerning doing some NLP consulting with them. I asked them how they would realize that the two days had been a great success. One of them said it would have a 'feel-good factor' and, at the same time, made a signal with two hands towards his stomach. At the point when I practiced the words 'feel great factor' to him, he gestured in confirmation. Later on, I referred to the great vibe factor, and all the while utilized his gesture. Rather than a nod of confirmation, I got a full physiological reaction, including skin coloring changes, stance and energy changes... the full works. His words had been a good anchor, yet the words in addition to the gesture were far more complete. At the point when I utilized both, I got a full reaction. I kept on utilizing the stay all through the meeting. At no time was he aware that I was utilizing NLP and his stays – he simply had the experience of being well understood. You can utilize NLP stays to catch and re-utilize positive experiences for yourself as well as other people. Presently have a go at doing this NLP practice as well...

1. Think of an event when you had a highly pleasurable, positive, or enjoyable experience. See what you saw at that point (watching out through your own

eyes), hear what you heard and feel what you felt. As you feel the sensations increase in intensity, squeeze the thumb and index finger of your left hand delicately together for a couple of seconds, at that point, release them. Presently 'break your state' (E.g., by remembering what shoe you put on first today.) Squeeze your thumb and pointer together once more, gently beating them. The state will return.

2. Identify something that somebody you realize as of now does, and make a subtle anchor. Set the stay while they are doing the activity. Later, fire your NLP anchor and see what occurs. If they do the thing you anchored, at that point, it worked!

3. When you (or somebody you are with) are experiencing something, you need to have a greater amount of anchor.

Not usual, remember that this stuff is amazing, so utilize your NLP skills wisely. Also, allow yourself to begin getting awareness of when it is being utilized on you. Promoters, government officials, and stand-up entertainers all know the power of NLP stays and use them with great cunning (and to great impact.) Awareness with NLP is the key – have a lot of fun.

Technique 17: Using empath skills

It could be your pass to a better life.

What is an empath? An empath resembles a wipe that absorbs the entirety of the feelings and vitality around them. They can tell when somebody close to them is feeling disturbed or angry without walking with them.

While this is an amazing ability, it can also accompany its downsides. Much like a wipe doesn't find a good pace it absorbs, an empath is powerless against absorbing any negativity that encompasses them. A nice day can rapidly transform into one loaded up with anxiety.

In any case, there are approaches to utilize your empathic skills to further your potential benefit and improve your day by day life. Here's the ticket.

1. Transform bad vibes into a good strategy.

In case you're an empath, think about the vibes and the feelings you get as data. The more data you have available to you, the more intelligent decisions you can make.

The world is made out of relationships, and realizing how to explore the people you come into contact with is an enormous piece of being effective. Rub a wrong person the incorrect way, and you may very well suffer a serious setback. Join your emotional insight into your life procedure.

2. Get on issues before they become bad dreams.

It is certainly a torment to take on others' negative feelings, yet it's not all bad! Numerous individuals get blindsided by significant issues and can't deal with them appropriately.

As an empath, you can get on potential issues before they arrive at their peak. Possibly you've begun to see that there is an irregular measure of the tension between two of your friends, for instance. Utilize your empathic capacities by diffusing the circumstance before it turns into a bad dream, or by setting yourself up for the eventual fallout.

3. Improve your relationships.

If your closest friend, significant other, or a family member has been radiating aggressive or sad vibes lately, accept that as a signal for you to step in and show at least a bit of kindness to heart. Perhaps you accidentally upset them, and as opposed to going up against you about it, they are harboring negative emotions toward you.

It is consistently to further everybody's potential benefit to let some circulation into complaints and keep a strong and honest line of communication. Your empathic capacities can improve your relationship if you make sense of how to decipher others' feelings and acceptable behavior on them.

4. Improve your work relationships

Your empathic nature can improve your work relationships similarly as it can your relationships. Workplaces can be wild and distressing. Getting many individuals to cooperate easily and work on the page can be difficult. That is the reason it is in every case best that you realize what is happening around you and how to associate with your coworkers and bosses.

An empath will get on any anxiety in the workplace, which can regularly negatively affect their feelings or even their work performance. However, knowing the condition of your workplace can assist you in getting through the day unscathed. It can also assist you in relating better to your fellow workers.

5. Prepare yourself for a tough road ahead.

An empath will have the option to tell when things at work or things in their relationship are not working out positively. If you begin to feel a feeling of fear or premonition, you can start setting yourself up for awful news before it shows up.

If you sense that your workplace has gotten more unfriendly of late, or that your partner has been uniquely removed, it might be a great opportunity to detail a course of action. That way, if life gets ugly, you'll be prepared to take difficulties head-on.

6. Prepare yourself to move on.

Another positive that comes with having the option to set yourself up for bad news is that it can empower you to proceed onward more rapidly and all the more no problem at all. Losing your employment or your relationship is continually going to hurt, yet if you can see it preceding it occurs, you can accelerate your recovery timeline.

The sooner you perceive a proverbial runaway train traveling in your direction, the sooner you can escape the way and keep an eye on your wounds. It's not exactly how you handle a significant difficulty, yet how you can proceed onward and gain from it.

7. Help another person sort through their feelings.

One of the most satisfying feelings comes with realizing you have helped somebody. Since empaths can read others' feelings, they additionally can assist people with managing those feelings.

Somebody close to you may be feeling discouraged, yet nobody else has gotten on it or has tried to talk with them about it. If you can detect what another person is experiencing, you can be the individual who goes to their guide. Improving another person's life or even just another person's day is extremely rewarding.

8. Transform feeling into understanding.

There is a difference between being aware of something and having the option to get something. An empath may feel others' feelings. However, that won't help anybody very much if they can't get them.

Figuring out how to transform perception into information and information energetically is what it's everything about. If you have empathic capacities, use them! It doesn't need to be only an uninvolved aptitude or a weight. Your common capacities as an empath can make you a superior individual if you let them.

Technique 18: How to use Deception.

Double-dealing refers to the demonstration—huge or little, cruel or kind—of making somebody think something that is false. Indeed, even commonly fair individuals practice deception; different examinations show that the normal individual lies a few times each day. A portion of those lies are huge ("I've never cheated on you!"); however, more frequently, they are little white lies ("That dress looks fine") sent to avoid uncomfortable situations or extra somebody's emotions.

Deception isn't constantly an outward-facing act. There are also the lies people let themselves know, for reasons running from the strong support of confidence to severe delusions outside their ability to control. While lying oneself is commonly seen as harmful, a few specialists argue that specific sorts of self-deception—like trusting one can achieve a difficult goal regardless of whether proof exists despite what might be expected—can positively affect by and large prosperity.

Trust is the bedrock of public activity at all levels, from romance and parenting to national government. Double-dealing constantly undermines it.

Is It Possible to Spot a Liar?

Specialists have since quite a while ago looked for approaches to definitively detect when somebody is lying. One of the best and well-known techniques, the polygraph test, depends on the hypothesis that lying adjusts typical psychophysiology designs that can be detected by sensitive machinery. Although mainstream in crime shows and films, the test has, for quite some time, been questionable, with no proof that there are conclusive variances in physiology. Proof recommends that those with certain mental issues, as Antisocial Personality Disorder, can't be precisely estimated by a polygraph or other normal lie-detection methods.

Numerous specialists propose that liars reveal themselves in "tells," major and minor changes in non-verbal communication or facial expressions. However, proof shows that such observable signs of lying can be unreliable and that double-dealing recognition—even by clinicians—is no more prominent than a possibility.

Location of double-dealing, but is basic for law authorization, and the quest for strong techniques is continuous. Many interested parties have moved their concentrate away from outward signs of deceiving the utilization of meeting strategies that reveal lying. Research indicates that, in key circumstances, the number of words one uses, just as the kind of words and the repetition of words, would all be able to help trained interviewers detect deception.

Why We Lie

Nobody likes being deceived, and when open figures are caught in a lie, it can turn into a significant scandal. In any case, while numerous individuals value trustworthy honesty—and try to separate themselves from people who are more comfortable with deceptions—truly everybody lies, for a variety of reasons. A few specialists propose that a specific measure of deception might be vital for keeping up a sound, working society.

The formal study of deception was before the space of ethicists and scholars, however more as of late, clinicians have directed their attention toward why individuals lie and the conditions that make them bound to do as such.

Technique 19: Use the right Gestures

Non-verbal communication is a fundamental piece of human association, since we impart through non-verbal communication, regardless of whether explicitly or implicitly. It is a piece of non-verbal communication and certainly uncovers aims and perspectives for those people who can understand them. Non-verbal communication assumes a pronounced job in the charisma of men and women, and having the option to utilize it deliberately and knowing about its expressiveness can fill in as an incredible advantage. In this way, it is attractive to learn NLP, and along these lines, gain information about non-verbal communication.

In the following content, non-verbal communication is clarified in more detail and made clearer using examples. Run of the mill practices and their expressiveness will be featured and clarified, including where they originate from and why they are demonstrated.

Body language – Definition

Body language includes all types of gestures, postures and body movements - from the handshake to sitting position and stance, situating of arms, legs, and feet, playing with hands, fingers and items, head act, and the various types of the eye to eye connection, just as distance behavior.

Interpreting body language

The following table shows a delegate model for significant areas of body language to give a first excellent introduction to the translation of body language. Along these lines, other brief activities are interpreted and explained by describing human behaviors as uncovered by the body start to finish.

Head

The most evident type of body language happens at the head, all the more correctly in the face, facial expressions. Run of the mill and recognizable facial expressions are wrinkled forehead or causing a commotion. The last proposes shock or a kind of contempt.

The lips pass on non-verbal significance. In the disposition of the sides of the mouth, regardless of whether they are pulled up in a smile or fall sadly, can demonstrate the perspective of an inattentive person. However, these facial features can be better controlled intentionally. Oblivious, and accordingly wild since they result from a sort of biofeedback, are dry lips. A saturating of the lips is consequently to be interpreted as an indication of apprehension or energy.

Neck

From the perspective of development, the neck is viewed as a powerless body part and along these lines uncovers much about one's perspective, regardless of whether one feels comfort or discomfort. At the point when an individual covers his neck by pulling the head back and chin in, or by setting their hands to their necks, it very well may be considered as a protective reflex or expression of discomfort. If the individual shows uncovered the neck, e.g., by tilting the head, it recommends that he feels good in the circumstance, or trusts his partner.

Shoulders/Torso

The shoulders and middle are liable for body act. It is commonly notable that: an upright posture, with shoulders back, outstretched chest, and a straight trunk, is viewed as an indication of certainty. The opposite doesn't constantly mean that an individual doesn't have confidence, because for reasons of comfort, and increasingly contracted posture is regularly taken when sitting in one spot for a more drawn out timeframe. As a rule, however, an upright posture appears to be more grounded and presents a more favorable appearance.

Hands

The hands are not just significant for reading non-verbal communication given their signals, yet also, since how and where they are held, if there is no obvious interaction, deceive much about an individual. One of the primary exercises of giving introductions is signaling. All that is said ought to be supported by gestures. This explains the expectation and underlines the significance of the delivered message.

Also, the utilization of gestures is seen as satisfying to the audience, as it makes a talk progressively striking and along these lines simpler to follow. But, it is significant not just what the speaker does with his hands while he is talking, yet additionally while he is quiet. Covered up, collapsed hands radiate uncertainty and discomfort. An open, spread hand act, for example, the "Merkel jewel" (fingertips squeezed together, thumbs inverse and squeezed together), communicates certainty. This hand motion can be valuable in exchange, for instance, since it radiates security and causes the other individual to feel more comfortable.

Legs/Feet

The legs can also say a great deal regarding comfort or discomfort when sitting. At the point when an individual is nervous, for instance, in a prospective employee meet-up, this can be demonstrated by eager legs. This is uncovered, entomb alia, by the way that the legs somewhat rock or swing, or the situation of the legs is regularly changed.

The feet are viewed as the most legit part of the human body. From the situating of the feet, an individual will frequently uncover his intentions. At the point when the two feet point at the other individual in a discussion, this means the individual is giving close attention to the next and is keen on the discussion. Conversely, directing one of the two feet toward the door means that the individual needs to end the discussion. Also, affection can be uncovered by the feet. In this way, when couples "foot" one another, it proposes that the relationship is intact and romantic.

Body language in men and women

The belief that people have extraordinary non-verbal communication is a mistake. Non-verbal communication is all-inclusive and contrasts between people, however not in general between a man and a lady. Because of gender roles, people do show various practices, yet non-verbal communication signals continue as before. The little contrasts that exist will be examined in the following section.

The body language of flirting

This section details how people show each other their love and how to interpret well-known signals.

A fundamental guideline in being a flirting says: Whatever you feel, they feel. Our body has a pronounced system of purportedly reflected neurons. This means when we perceive how somebody plays out some activity, similar neurons fire as though we were doing the activity ourselves. In this way, it is to be expected that the other person in a flirt feels similarly.

Fundamentally being a tease includes the ideas of comfort and discomfort revealed in the particular responses as effectively described. When the other individual feels good, he additionally shows this when being a flirting through the run of the typical expressions. However, in flirting, one must separate between a man and a lady. Ladies will, in general, show interest in playful, agreeable motions, for example, playing with the hair or biting the lip. Men, in any case, give clear indications of comfort, yet also signs that can be mistaken for discomfort, as they can provide indications of nervousness when strongly pulled in to a lady.

At long last, moreover the idea of comfort, two different signs are to be interpreted as away from affection: strong eye to eye connection and, as depicted in the past section, the feet of the other individual.

The body language of lying

Lying is regularly connected with body language because our eye development and the association of facial expressions and gestures can tell our partner if we are lying or talking reality. That is the reason why reading the body language of a liar is so interesting. It should initially be noticed that lying frequently occurs with regards to an unfortunate circumstance, for example, when under addressing, and along these lines, the individual feels stress and discomfort. These signs of stress and anxiety are identical to the commonplace practices that happen when lying. This makes it even harder to reveal a liar and includes the risk of falsely accusing a human being of lying. Thus, it is critical to place the presumed liar in a lovely, agreeable temperament before cross-examination to keep the conflicting stress factors as low as could be expected under the circumstances.

Moreover, it ought to be noticed that there are not any general practices of liars. Or maybe, they can fluctuate between individuals. In any case, there are as yet a couple of components that can show for a liar. Keeping away from the eye to eye connection and frequent blinking can mean that the suspected liar is reluctant to be afraid by prolonged eye to eye connection. A fixed look or rolling of the eyes are not run of the mill practices that result from simple pressure or anxiety yet is usually a sign of discomfort.

Undoubtedly, attention ought to be paid to the implicit response to the questions. If limbs suddenly stop moving after a question, this may imply that the interviewee feels got. Also, scratching, redness of the face, and an exaggerated facial expression might be proof that he has something to cover up. However, every one of these signs and a lot more that are communicated in other non-verbal channels, there is no all-inclusive supernatural occurrence technique for exposing liars. Here, empathy and tact are expected to get reality out of someone else.

Improving body language

Body language is an expansive theme in which individuals in numerous areas have directed research. Familiarity with what signal can create which impact can provide an individual with numerous advantages, not simply at work or in an association, however, in all everyday issues.

Improving body language not just causes individuals to appear to be more self-assured and affable; it also encourages them to feel better naturally.

Technique 20: How to use Charisma

Charisma isn't only for celebrities. It's a social quality that anybody can create.

Consider charisma, power of character, or personal presence, or gravitas.

Individuals with more significant levels of charisma will, in general, be seen, tuned in to, regarded, and followed.

A strong charismatic personal presence is helpful for driving, instructing, selling, talking, and connections of different types. Having an appealing power of character is also helpful for defending yourself as well as other people, and for arranging, griping, and looking for a change - particularly when coordinated to a higher authority or somebody who believes they're superior to you.

Charismatic power isn't regularly instructed. However, it tends to be.

Charismatic to the Core is the great new book about authentic leadership by Nikki Owen. Nikki is a specialist in charisma - in the worth and importance of charisma forever, work, authority, and so forth. Furthermore, how to turn out to be more charismatic. Nikki has examined and redefined charisma to be a quantifiable, substantial, learnable quality. She clarifies and trains charisma with the goal that it is a profound and advanced perspective on humankind and credibility, significant to every one of us.

The thought that charisma is 'God-given' owes a lot to oneself, securing thoughts of the historical ruling classes.

Rulers, leaders, and organizations all through the ages would, in general, keep up power by convincing everybody (counting themselves) that standard individuals had neither the privilege nor the capacity to achieve any sort of greatness. To differing degrees, individuals in power, and certain foundations and companies can even now be seen acting right now.

An appeal, and other incredible human characteristics like service, information, and wisdom, were verifiably the preserve of the first class and those alongside God - past the desires of normal individuals. Some accept this still to be so.

In the meantime, however, the cutting edge age is making everything possible for everybody.

Most 'leaders' are currently supporters, chasing patterns, and popularity. Customary individuals achieve significance consistently. Circumstances are different and keep on changing, ceaselessly from old-style dictator structures and beliefs. Individuals are perpetually engaged.

In the advanced age, 'standard,' individuals progressively realize that they can achieve anything they need.

Becoming charismatic - like turning out to be whatever else you need to be - is never again a blessing from the divine beings or an elegant training. If you need to be charming, you can be.

Why charisma?

Charisma is firmly identified with emphatics, which we as a whole need, if just for protective reasons. An appeal isn't just about showing off.

Charisma empowers us to impact (and rouse) others, and to impact our extreme condition, which every once in a while we as a whole need to do - even the thoughtful people among us. Time the board, for instance, crucially depends upon dealing with our condition and the desires for other people.

If you need to manufacture a business, lead a group, be an educator or a teacher or a speaker, or perhaps enter legislative issues, at that point, you have more explanations behind building up your attractive forces.

Charisma isn't consistently a production that only special people possess. Charisma is a power of human character which can be understood, estimated, and created. And keeping in mind that a few people appear to be more ordinarily appealing than others, in all truth anybody - given effort and belief - can create charming force, either as a conscious behavior to be utilized when required or as a deeper 'natural.'

Charisma helps move others, driving a group, or educating and creating individuals, or being an innovator or a fund-raiser.

Charisma is additionally useful for venturing to the board, critical thinking, facilitating, and spearheading.

Also, the allure is helpful for a wide range of individual connections - dating, mating, parenting, etc. Charisma helps in any circumstance where you need or need to impact others and external factors.

At the point when you see the charm in these terms - and as a method for understanding and controlling your quality of character - you may also observe reasons in your own life for needing to build up some appealing power for yourself.

Technique 21: How to utilize Leadership

Leadership: NLP for Leaders – what affects?

Numerous business Leaders perceive the additional worth that NLP brings to a variety of business exercises, and they also esteem NLP for their proficiency and self-improvement. Leaders, Executives, and Business Owners are consistently watching out for improvement opportunities that help them, or their groups become more persuasive communicators, mentors, coaches, time supervisors, and ability spotters, managers of progress, and people developers. What all Leaders and Managers share for all intents and purpose is their longing to more better understand and support their groups to create and to assist them with being as well as can be expected be (and we're all watching out for approaches to show signs of improvement results, all the more effectively or successfully, right?).

NLP for Business Leadership

What might you get if you combined a gifted and skillful technical professional with a compelling and skilled Leader? (No, this isn't the beginning of a joke!) – what you would get is somebody who is incredibly important to a business association as they would have the option to utilize their specialized skills on an individual level while additionally giving guidance and authority at an organizational level. Everybody can be a leader, and in actuality, we are all as of now leaders – continually impacting the individuals and occasions around us – our friends, associates, colleagues, and our 'tribes.' Anyway, in associations you frequently observe specialized experts being advanced, and here and there they battle with the impacting, conveying and relationship building abilities required to be a Business Leader or Manager (I've met numerous leaders and directors who concede that a portion of the more subtle, softer skills are not their strength). Our experience shows that those associations who put resources into the softer skills of the individuals they utilize in administrative and influential positions become more productive, forward-looking, and industry-driving. Incorporating NLP into your initiative tool compartment will empower you to build up the abilities, the viewpoint, and the social adaptability with which to improve your presentation in a world of flatter corporate structures, cross-utilitarian duties, complex connections, focused on workforces, and neighborhood and remote group work. To exceed expectations, the managers and leaders of today require inconspicuous abilities that incorporate having the option to propel and truly work to get the best out of the people they lead. It requires a unique skill set that NLP can offer.

In business, NLP gives first devices in many vital areas, including:

- Communicating skillfully with peers, direct reports, and with senior management. Build up Rapport with anybody (Rapport being the basis of all communication). Listen deeply. Present utilizing clear incredible language and a configuration or structure that will interest everybody in your crowd.

- Help Leaders gain clarity over what they need – imperative for giving a precise and reliable course

- Understand the foundational idea of communication with and inside groups – including the inconspicuous elements of non-verbal impact

- Understand the reasoning and emotional make-up of groups and the people inside these groups – and of the way where these people arrange

- Gain new bits of knowledge into circumstances and connections utilizing 'Perceptual Positions' (an NLP instrument also used to resolve conflict and produce new thoughts or viewpoints)

- Understand oneself, figure out how to deal with your feelings and have increased self-aware

- Model the successful practices of others so they can be repeated

- Understand the job of beliefs and qualities in what is most important to individuals
- Know how to use esteems to tailor the inspirational way to deal with suit every person
- Setting convincing objectives and moving individuals by 'selling' them the group or organizational vision and getting their 'buy-in' to this vision
- Acquire the attitudes and beliefs that support the sure authority
- Influence the workplace with the goal that it encourages individuals to be useful and beneficial.

Technique 22: Fake it until you make it

At some point, a customer came to see me since she felt socially bad. She realized that her failure to make small talk was holding her back both personally and professionally. As a timid individual, she hated going to systems networking events. But, making associations was essential to her career. I asked, "What do you generally do when you go to a networking event?" She stated, "I stand clumsily off to the side and hold back to check whether anybody will come to talk with me." I asked her, "What might you do any other way if you felt sure?" and she stated, "I'd start a discussion and introduce myself with individuals."

At that moment, she found the answer to her concern: If she needed to feel more confident, she needed to act more confident. That wasn't exactly what she needed to hear. She'd sought after an answer that would quickly cause her to feel more satisfied. But, the way to getting more agreeable in social circumstances is practice.

Acting "As if"

Acting "as if" is an ideal solution in psychotherapy. It depends on the possibility that if you carry on like the individual you need to become, you'll become like this as a general rule:

- If you need to feel happier, do what happy individuals do—smell.
- If you need to complete more work, go about as though you are a productive person.

- If you need to have more friends, carry on like a friendly individual.
- If you need to improve your relationship, work on being the right partner.

Over and over again, we falter to get a move on. Rather, we hold up until everything feels perfect or until we believe we're prepared. But, exploration shows that changing your behavior initially can change how you think and feel.

The Biggest Mistake Most People Make

Faking it until you make it possibly works when you correctly identify something inside yourself that is keeping you down. Behaving on like the individual you need to become is tied in with changing how you feel and how you think. If your thought processes are to demonstrate your value to others, in any case, your efforts won't be effective and exploration shows that this methodology backfires. An examination distributed in the Journal of Consumer Research found that people who attempted to demonstrate their value to others were bound to harp on their shortcomings. Aggressive professionals who wore luxury apparel with an end goal to seem useful, and MBA students who wore Rolex watches to build their self-esteem simply wound up feeling like bigger failures.

How to "Fake It" the Right Way

Acting "as if" doesn't mean being fake or inauthentic. It's tied in with changing your behavior first and believing the feelings will follow. For whatever length of time that your motivation is in the ideal spot, faking it until you cause it to can viably cause your objectives to become a reality. Simply ensure you're keen on changing yourself on the inside, not just trying to change others' views of you.

Technique 23: Never stop train yourself

There are five essential ways that Neuro-Linguistic Programming can help change yourself and your life to improve things.

Learning to dissociate yourself

Passionate pressure has a habit of expending us. Whenever left unaddressed, the negative feelings can consume you and keep you from proceeding to develop and succeed.

Neuro-Linguistic Programming can assist you with killing these emotions and allow you to see the situation objectively. Rather than getting angry and frustrated as a response to push, you'll figure out how to disassociate yourself from the negativity.

Re-frame the content

In circumstances where you feel feeble and are powerless by feelings, the procedure of "content reframing" can help switch your focus and reduce the stress, therefore. In all circumstances, there are certain and negative angles. By changing your view, you can turn off the negative aspects and feature the advantages that have created, therefore.

Anchor yourself

Another procedure is to anchor a positive emotional reaction, even amidst an exceptionally stressful circumstance. By intentionally diverting a positive emotional state, similar to satisfaction or courage, you're ready to modify how you are feeling at that specific minute.

Learn to build rapport

Is Life about communication and connections, right? NLP encourages you to master the ability of compatibility building, which can be pertinent in both expert and personal situations. You'll figure out how to interface with a person through their breathing examples, non-verbal communication, and discussion. You'll figure out how to focus on the individual, utilize comparable words, and even mirror their body language to manufacture a stronger rapport.

Expose your limiting beliefs

All through a specialist certification course, you will identify and uncover the limiting beliefs that are keeping you away from achieving your objectives. By understanding these negative emotions, you'll have the option to change them into substantially more positive thoughts. This knowledge is one of the most remarkable neuro-linguistic procedures you'll pick up as your perspectives will eventually decide how you carry on with your life and what you'll achieve.

At last, this sort of training causes you to create devices to deal with the stressors throughout your life. The methods you gain all through an eight-day course, for instance, will assist you with figuring out how to communicate effectively, resolve conflicts and understand the convictions and practices that are preventing you from achieving your personal and professional goals.

5·

THE BASICS OF DECEPTION

Deception is an unpredictable social behavior that includes a lot of higher psychological capacities. Studying this essential wonder in people has, in all ages, been driven not only by the desire to understand the basic system of mental working but instead by the ambition to detect deceptive behavior in criminal suspects. In this way, recognizing legitimate pointers of deceptive behavior has consistently been in the focal point of deception research. Such pointers can be characterized as far as explicit behavior, physiological corresponds, or substance of verbal reports. The subject of how validly every pointer takes into account separating honest and beguiling records is characteristic in most of the research efforts in this domain.

Another significant perspective concerns the advancement of deception theory. As indicated by current feelings, deception isn't described by a single subjective procedure yet instead includes the mix of a variety of essential psychological procedures, for example, working memory, reaction monitoring, and inhibition. Recognizing these procedures, demonstrating their interplay and their regulation by character and situational factors, is as yet one significant challenge in deception research. Moreover, double-dealing is no unitary wonder. Correspondingly, researchers need to analyze and depict various variations of this wonderful happening in particular settings, which involves a variety of exploratory and hypothetical methodologies that, to a great extent, differ in scope and techniques.

Current Interests

One significant field in deception research concerns the utilization of psychophysiological techniques to detect deceptive behavior. After some time, the traditional physiological measures (electro-dermal, cardiovascular, and respiratory reactions) have been enhanced by electroencephalographic, utilitarian imaging, and other innovative methodologies. Discovering measures that truly separate among truth and lie, and the desire to optimize their utilization, have gotten new impulse from recent technological development. Neuroimaging strategies, for instance, yield new guarantees and deserve a deep evaluation. Warm imaging and eye-tracking are other innovative techniques that may give extra data about the psychological procedures associated with producing deceptive reactions. But, even "great" social estimates, for example, reaction times are still much of the time utilized right now hypothetical just as applied purposes.

Various strategies for detecting deception with the assistance of physiological measures have been disputably examined in the scientific community. Among the most compelling trial standards, the supposed Concealed Information Test has gotten expansive logical consideration. The CIT doesn't focus on identifying double-dealing in essence but instead targets identifying whether a suspect has disguised information on explicit (e.g., crime-related) details. An alternate methodology is the so-called differentiation-of-deception paradigm, which follows the means to recognize explicit examples in conduct or physiological factors that vary methodically among truthful and deceptive behavior. Especially this last methodology has been recently filled by brain imaging systems, which guarantee to reflect mental procedures going with deceptive responses more directly.

The flow Research Topic unites commitments from exploratory brain science, psychophysiology, and neuroscience, focusing on the understanding of the expansive idea of misdirection, including the location of covered data, as for essential research questions just as applied issues. Because of the interdisciplinary focus of this methodology, articles were distributed in Frontiers in Psychology or Frontiers in Human Neuroscience, individually.

6.

BONUS: TIPS FROM THE AUTHOR'S EXPERIENCE

1. Tell a good story.

Clinicians examining the account structure reveal to us that people are great storytellers. The story fits the human mind quickly, and language presumably created to some extent for us to recount stories to one another. Try to make your diary article a convincing story. You are addressing an interesting issue or phenomenon, utilizing speculations created to clarify the issues. You have propelled hypotheses, created techniques to test them, if results bearing on the problems, and then interpreted the outcomes considering the theories and hypotheses. You arrived at a satisfying resolution, propelling information. Experiments regularly try to unravel a puzzle, and puzzles make for good stories. On the whole, your article ought to have a strong storyline. Give an easily remembered take-home message. You ought to give clear responses to the following two questions the reader will have: What has the paper revealed to me that I didn't know previously? Also, for what reason is this news significant?

2. Try not to have an excessive number of subplots.

You may wish to disclose to some subsidiary stories, moreover your primary plot, because your informational index may allow you to address different focuses. However, don't have too much. I took in this exercise in graduate school. One of my fellow students directed a progression of examinations and thought of them up for his tutor (Endel Tulving) to consider for joint production. The student wrote a paper that had nine primary concerns dependent on a few analyses. Tulving gave it back, saying a paper would never have more than three primary concerns since readers would throw up their hands and not waste time with the entire thing. In any case, the student said that each of the nine was similarly significant and must be incorporated. They went to and fro for some time; however, the outcome was that the paper — which had new information — was rarely distributed. If you think a progression of investigations has numerous accounts to tell, break them into smaller chunks.

3. Create an outline.

Before you start writing, make a diagram of your paper, particularly for the presentation and general discussion. What are the focuses basically for the introduction? What is the rationale you are working on for your examination? The strategy is typically direct, with the outline gave. A diagram is valuable for the outcomes if they are at all complicated. You have to think about the request for an introduction. Should information be introduced in tables, figures, or in the content? The general discussion needs a clear outline, so it doesn't wander. Work in the principal passage of the public discussion to condense the essential findings of the paper. You have to summarize the key findings before talking about them, and numerous readers seek that passage for the news in your paper.

4. Provide a good title.

Most readers skimming the chapter by chapter guide on the web or in a diary will take a look at the title, and the writers' names and (if you are lucky) will read your concept. There is no way around the names (no, you can't include a famous psychologist long deceased); however, you can control your title and your abstract. Titles come in numerous flavors, yet four essential ones ring a bell. A necessary kind is of the structure "Impacts of the free factor on the dependent variable." There is nothing wrong with this kind of title, and the more significant part of us have utilized it now and again. But, these titles don't jump out at the reader, saying, "read me now." Another sort of title gives a one-sentence theoretical of what the paper found. From a 2006 issue of Psychonomic Bulletin and Review comes "Individuals more than 40 feel 20 percent more youthful than their age: Subjective age over the life expectancy" by David Rubin and Dorthe Berntsen. Indeed, even without the caption, the essential piece of the title passes on the content of the story. Scholastics also love to utilize colons in their titles, as right now. The colon assists with getting your story across because you find good pace words. You can express the general point before the colon and add to it a short time later. Here is an interesting example from an ongoing Psychological Science article by Brad Bushman and a few partners: "When God sanctions killing: Effect of scriptural violence on hostility." With a title that way, it's hard not to in any event read the dynamic, if not the entire paper.

CONCLUSION

Such a large number of individuals (counting the individuals who normally read the Psychology Today magazine) trust psychologists with their emotional, social, instructive, and social well-being and health. They should be sure that psychologists consistently make the best choice and follow these significant moral standards no matter what. It might require some time and effort to recover that considerable trust. But, ideally, the organization has been awakened to do as such and do as such with extraordinary force. There's motivation to accept that the journey for happiness could be a way to hopelessness. Considers have discovered that the more value people place on happiness, the less glad they become. You see, when we need to be happy, we search for strong positive feelings like delight, happiness, energy, and enthusiasm, and tragically; essentially, these feelings will, in general, be short-lived. With an end goal to secure these emotions, we will, in general, overestimate the effect of our conditions, invest a lot of energy comparing our current happiness with our past joy, and we become too self-centered. If you figure you might be engaged with a Dark Triad character, look for psychotherapy. Try not to be afraid to talk with others about your experience. Covering up bad behavior is a typical yet risky type of refusal. Find out about narcissistic abuse, subtle types of misuse, damaging connections, and narcissistic connections. Figure out How to Be Assertive and Peruse Dealing with a Narcissist. Violence has gone before by psychological abuse. If you've been threatened with savagery, don't sit tight for it to occur or believe that it won't be repeated. Dark Psychology places some individuals who commit these same acts and do so, not for influence, cash, sex, revenge, or some other known reason. They submit horrid acts without an objective. Rearranged, their finishes don't legitimize their methods. Some individuals damage and harm others for doing as such. Inside every last one of us is this potential. A possibility to hurt others without cause, clarification, or design is the area explored. Dark Psychology accepts this dim potential is more complex and much more challenging to define.